# Cambridge Elements

Elements in Global Humanities
edited by
Saul Dubow
*University of Cambridge*
Malvika Maheshwari
*Ashoka University*
Frisbee C. C. Sheffield
*University of Cambridge*

# ESOTERIC ORIENTALISM

## Mandakini Dubey
*Ashoka University*

CAMBRIDGE
UNIVERSITY PRESS

Shaftesbury Road, Cambridge CB2 8EA, United Kingdom

One Liberty Plaza, 20th Floor, New York, NY 10006, USA

477 Williamstown Road, Port Melbourne, VIC 3207, Australia

314–321, 3rd Floor, Plot 3, Splendor Forum, Jasola District Centre,
New Delhi – 110025, India

103 Penang Road, #05–06/07, Visioncrest Commercial, Singapore 238467

Cambridge University Press is part of Cambridge University Press & Assessment,
a department of the University of Cambridge.

We share the University's mission to contribute to society through the pursuit of
education, learning and research at the highest international levels of excellence.

www.cambridge.org
Information on this title: www.cambridge.org/9781009630023

DOI: 10.1017/9781009630030



When citing this work, please include a reference to the DOI 10.1017/9781009630030

First published 2025

*A catalogue record for this publication is available from the British Library*

ISBN 978-1-009-63002-3 Hardback
ISBN 978-1-009-63006-1 Paperback
ISSN 3049-821X (online)
ISSN 3049-8201 (print)

Cambridge University Press & Assessment has no responsibility for the persistence
or accuracy of URLs for external or third-party internet websites referred to in this
publication and does not guarantee that any content on such websites is, or will remain,
accurate or appropriate.

For EU product safety concerns, contact us at Calle de José Abascal, 56, 1°, 28003
Madrid, Spain, or email eugpsr@cambridge.org

# Esoteric Orientalism

Elements in Global Humanities

DOI: 10.1017/9781009630030
First published online: June 2025

Mandakini Dubey
*Ashoka University*

**Author for correspondence:** Mandakini Dubey,
mandakini.dubey@ashoka.edu.in

**Abstract:** *Esoteric Orientalism* studies Victorian esotericism and academic Orientalism as the nineteenth century's most significant comparative frameworks for understanding global religions, languages, and cultures. Occultist formations like the Theosophical Society (led by Helena Petrovna Blavatsky) and Orientalist disciplines like philology and comparative religion (as exemplified by Friedrich Max Müller) both believed in the essential kinship of East and West, routed through the Aryan family hypothesis – generating new visions of race and caste even while expanding the category of self. Still, theosophy and philology shared a contentious relationship. Blavatsky's writings anticipate postcolonial commentary in critiquing Orientalist scholarly presumption; her fantastical citational practices hold a mortifying mirror to academic Orientalism. Above all, the Element traces how heterogeneous, riven, and powerfully consequential the larger discourse of Orientalism could be. *Esoteric Orientalism* combines broad historical narrative with literary close reading, recasting Theosophy as a speculative and imaginative construct through which to read Orientalist discourse more broadly.

**Keywords:** theosophy, Friedrich Max Müller, Helena Petrovna Blavatsky, Aryan, occultism



ISBNs: 9781009630023 (HB), 9781009630061 (PB), 9781009630030 (OC)
ISSNs: 3049-821X (online), 3049-8201 (print)

# Contents

# 1 Introduction

"Orientalism" is the closest we come to a name for the global humanities in the eighteenth and nineteenth centuries, a time when much of the interdisciplinary, transcultural study of history, society, and philosophy took place under its rubric. This Element turns to the late Victorian period, when questions and hypotheses thrown forth by preceding waves of imperial globalization crystallized into new or remade disciplines in the academic centers of the West. In its most technical sense, Orientalism refers to these scholarly disciplines, which developed through the work of translation in the colonies as well as in metropolitan academic centers.[1] The disciplines of Orientalism include comparative philology (impelled by the discovery of shared linguistic origins and language families across Europe and Asia), comparative religion (similarly fascinated by overlaps and differences among the world's faiths), and comparative ethnology (the study of peoples, races, and cultures). And yet, while it may seem that these scholarly disciplines were the only available contemporary avenue for the global humanities, other significant approaches also emerged alongside this scholarship. The occultist formations and movements of the Victorian period – most notably, the Theosophical Society – offered an alternative path of comparative, transcultural study, leading to what they described as the secret doctrine shared by the world's religious traditions. As this Element goes on to demonstrate, Victorian esotericism and Orientalism intersected with one another in relations that included consonance and derivation, rebuttal and disavowal, and antagonism as well as codependency. In attending closely to such points of overlap and the contentions they enabled, *Esoteric Orientalism* demonstrates the broader heterogeneity and incoherence of nineteenth-century colonial discourse.

At one level, of course, academic Orientalism and the occultist writings of the Theosophical Society are both part of the same broad spectrum of colonial discourse that also goes by the name of "Orientalism," since it assumes and replicates an essential dichotomy between the East and the West. The critical salience of the term clearly derives from Edward Said's epochal work, *Orientalism* (1978), which in many ways inaugurated the field of postcolonial theory with its suggestion that colonial structures of power cannot generate pure, disinterested cultural representations.[2] In Said's analysis, Orientalist

---

[1] As Urs App defines it, Orientalism in the modern sense is "the secular, institutionalized study of the Orient by specialists capable of understanding oriental languages and handling primary-source material" (App, *Birth*, p. xi).

[2] Harry Oldmeadow distinguishes between the epistemological-material complex as critiqued by Said, which he calls "Orientalism" with an uppercase "O," and the more value-neutral historic and ongoing involvement of Western scholars with the languages, religions, and so on of the East, which he terms "orientalism" with a lowercase "o" (Oldmeadow, *Journey*, p. 7).

knowledge embodies a form of mastery inseparable from the imperial power that enables it. In fact, it is a mastery that might be described as having invented its own object: "Knowledge of the Orient, because generated out of strength, in a sense creates the Orient, the Oriental, and his world."[3] As Said lays out his conceptual framework in *Orientalism*, he grants his key term a multiplicity of meanings, to match the various workings of power he sees in European representations of the Orient; many critics have gone on to question the neat alignment these meanings assume.[4] His broadest definition of Orientalism describes it as the process through which "the Occident" creates an internally consistent alter ego against which it might define itself. At the same time, this rather abstract psychoanalytical formulation incorporates materialist practices, since Said also understands Orientalism to mean, in Foucauldian terms, "the enormously systematic discipline by which European culture was able to manage ... the Orient politically, sociologically, militarily, ideologically, scientifically and imaginatively," as well as the material consequences of Orientalist constructions.[5] Ultimately, for Said, Orientalism does not simply name this form of "systematic discipline"; nor is it limited to the academic disciplines through which Western scholars sorted, classified, and translated the texts of the East. It is, also, more loosely, "a style of thought based upon an ontological and epistemological distinction made between 'the Orient' and ... 'the Occident.'"[6] As I will show in this Element, while that fundamental Orientalist "distinction" may seem rigidly essentialist, it accommodates implications in the plural, rather than the singular "style of thought" suggested by Said. Whereas occultists (such as Helena Petrovna Blavatsky, the cofounder of the Theosophical Society, who was also known as Madame Blavatsky or HPB) and Orientalists (such as the Indologist Friedrich Max Müller) both generally appear to assume "an ontological and epistemological distinction" between the East and the West in their writings, this by no means suggests homogeneity; in fact, they at times offer pointed and searing critiques of one another. Attending to such moments makes us aware of fissures and fault lines that run through the general terrain of colonial discourse.

A binary division such as the opposition of East and West seems to be a synchronic articulation, a cross-sectional snapshot of structure. The relation between Orient and Occident in this period, however, is also ineluctably diachronic, being saturated with a sense of time. This inescapable temporality

---

[3] Said, *Orientalism*, p. 40.

[4] See Oldmeadow's overview of significant interventions in the discourse and debates around Orientalism since Said for further leads on the important critics and texts through which to trace this conversation (Oldmeadow, *Journey*, p. 10).

[5] Said, *Orientalism*, p. 3.     [6] Said, *Orientalism*, p. 2.

asserts itself not only because we understand the dichotomy to be a product of history but also because it is itself a story about history. To bring together nineteenth-century writings by Orientalists and occultists is to view a temporal horizon that stretches in two directions, connecting the lost past of an originary racial, linguistic, and religious kinship among cultures – as first posited by Orientalist scholars – to a utopian future in which this essential, transcultural oneness might be repaired and revealed, as envisioned by Theosophy. The nineteenth-century present moment of these writings becomes then a bridge, and the opposition of East and West comes across more as a temporary phase or sublative turn than a fixed dichotomy: the twain have met, and the twain shall meet again. Whereas the Saidian view of the consequential dichotomy between the East and the West focuses on the force of distinction, the temporality we see in Orientalist and occultist narratives often presses in the direction of commonality.

Since the late eighteenth century, when William Jones postulated a long-vanished protolanguage that related Sanskrit and Persian to Latin and Greek (and so, to English and contemporary European languages), studying distant languages and religions became a way for Orientalists to compose an alternative history of the self, one that expanded from language to race and ethnicity. The notion of a family of languages acts in this time as a sign of ultimate kinship across differences. Even so, in the discourse around the linguistic family hypothesis (variously called "Indo-European" or "Aryan"), the plurality of races and cultures that together offer evidence of kinship also finds itself dispersed into further hierarchical relations, through narratives of degeneration and decline. As such, the "ontological and epistemological distinction" of which Said writes generates proliferating linguistic and racial taxonomies in this cultural moment, which in the Indian context also draws in the discourse of caste: These complexities are layered into the notion of shared kinship. Such intricacies show up differently in Orientalist and Theosophical writings, since the former operates within a framework of scholarly citations, while the latter sets forth a strange and sprawling esoteric cosmology that relies on the unquestioned authority of unverifiable sources. And yet, both Orientalism and Theosophy share significant questions and points of interest that complicate fundamental questions of racial and cultural kinship.

In this Element, the interrelation of Victorian Orientalism and occultism has the formal economy of a double helix. To trace it as such is to watch mutual influences and derivations twist and spiral into something altogether new. The hypothesis of an Indo-European protolanguage turns into the vision of an Aryan family reunion; philology gives way to the vocabulary of race science, and race science seemingly takes on the ring of revelation; a reliance on texts and archives dissolves into the fantasy of secret initiations and master teachers; and elaborate gradations of recondite orders and hierarchies seem to sublimate the logic of the caste system into a proliferating New Age esotericism. We will see that broadly theosophical impulses enlivened academic Orientalism even as Orientalism was intrinsic to the making of the Theosophical Society, despite the fact that their relationship was marked by vocal skepticism.[7] This formative relationship encoded several of the larger cultural preoccupations of the time; its effects have gone on to reverberate through different historical contexts.

As an Element in the Global Humanities, this Element follows these traces and reverberations back to a historical moment that put not just many cultures and but also many disciplines in conversation. In keeping with the larger remit of the global humanities, *Esoteric Orientalism* itself also embodies an interdisciplinary approach. As I write about Orientalist and Theosophical works from the late nineteenth century, I move freely between a broader, contextual narrative that places these texts in a history of ideas, and the close reading practices of literary and cultural studies. Piecing together the broad historical narrative allows us to follow the development, transformations, and crisscrossings of Orientalist and esotericist conceptions of language, religion, and race. At the same time, the telling of the story demands a closer attention to the forms, figures, syntax, and tropes of Theosophical and Orientalist discourse, to follow the constructions of (for example) race and caste at a granular and specific level. My approach is in keeping with Eve Kosofsky Sedgwick's conception of "reparative reading," as opposed to the project of exposure and wide explanation that she describes as "paranoid."[8] The postcolonial critique of Orientalist knowledge (as being inextricably implicated in the material project of imperialism) offers an x-ray of colonial discourse – it is, in Sedgwick's terms, a strong theory, which diagnoses deeply and explains widely. In recognizing Saidian postcolonial critique as paranoid, in Sedgwick's sense of the term, I am not censuring it: In fact, that critique is the foundation on which this study is built. But without in any way absolving Orientalist structures of knowledge of their investment in power relations, or neglecting their arrogations of authority, I will suggest through this Element that, read together closely and attentively, the writings of Orientalism and Theosophy reveal not just the self-transformations that followed from these

---

[7] The distinction between "theosophy" and "Theosophy" is indebted to Joscelyn Godwin's discussion of nineteenth-century movements in *The Theosophical Enlightenment*, as well as Antoine Faivre's broad overview of Boehmian theosophy in *Access to Western Esotericism*. As we see later in the Element, it is a distinction that we find mobilized by Max Müller, as well.

[8] See Eve Kosofsky Sedgwick, "Paranoid Reading and Reparative Reading, or, You're So Paranoid, You Probably Think This Essay Is about You."

global, transcultural encounters, or the contradictions and incoherencies within colonial discourse but also at times the self-consuming nature of its broadest claims to authority.[9]

The Element tells the complex story of this central relationship, beginning with the emergence of the Theosophical Society from the spiritualist milieu of the late nineteenth century, in which older traditions of Western occultism came into contact with ideas and texts unearthed by Orientalist scholarship. We see similar contact being made in the sci-fi novella with which I commence our discussion – Edward Bulwer-Lytton's *The Coming Race* (1871), which repeatedly engages conceptions of the Orient as well as the findings of philology as part of a broadly occultist imaginary. My reading of the novella focuses on the way that the genre's free-floating speculations and fantastical identifications cluster around this framework of allusions. In keeping with the Element's interdisciplinary method, this literary close reading leads into a broader history of the philological language family hypothesis and its racial implications, first as it took form in Orientalist scholarship over the eighteenth and nineteenth centuries, and then in Blavatsky's major works.

These early sections of the Element trace the overlaps between Orientalist scholarship and Blavatsky's (at times contradictory) views on fraught categories of identity such as race and caste. As I go on to demonstrate, the Theosophical Society's shift to India in 1879, its cofounders' interactions with Indian religious figureheads, and Blavatsky's claim to being initiated into the true meaning of religious texts by a secret fraternity of esoteric Himalayan "Masters," all bring a combative edge to these writings. Increasingly, the writings of Theosophy frame personal practice and spiritual initiation as an alternative to Orientalism's textual and "exoteric" bias – undermining the authoritative presumptions of academic Orientalists like Max Müller, and laying the ground for public sparring between Müller and the Theosophists. Finally, however, I suggest that Theosophy is not simply a source of critique for Orientalism: rather, its phantasmagoric adaptations from philology and comparative religion confront academic Orientalism with a reflection of fantasies within its own assumptions, identifications, and implications. Beyond their self-presentation as an alternative avenue of the global humanities, and beyond the binary of true and false, the writings of Theosophy demand to be read anew, as evocations of the speculative and the literary.

---

[9] Leela Gandhi reminds us to read Theosophy as a part of Western anti-imperialism, particularly as it flourished in the marginalized spaces of spiritualism, and enabled trans-cultural coalitions and bonds of the sort that we will explore while discussing the Theosophical Society's relationship with the Arya Samaj. See Gandhi, *Affective Communities.*

## 2 Excavating Esoteric Orientalism

While this Element focuses on the late nineteenth century, the history of Orientalism in relation to the occult would make for a much longer account. We see the foundations of such an account, for example, in Urs App's work in *The Birth of Orientalism* (2010). App argues against Said's central thesis, suggesting instead that "the role of colonialism (and generally of economic and political interests) in the birth of Orientalism dwindles to insignificance compared to the role of religion."[10] This polemical declaration seemingly sets religion aside from the realm of "economic and political interests" – a contestable separation, particularly during the colonial era, but App is writing primarily in relation to the early modern period. His approach also suggests that the Orientalists were impelled by a desire to locate common roots rather than the impulse to define oneself against an other. App's account gives esotericism a starring role in this early story, since he specifies "the distinction between 'outer' or 'exoteric' and 'inner' or 'esoteric' forms" as a key presence in this cultural encounter.[11] For instance, he tells us, Jesuit missionaries in the early modern period investigated and catalogued religious texts from around Asia in large part because they were taken by the notion of an occulted, mystical, and syncretic heart within the outer shell of religions like Buddhism, seeking a "pan-Asian 'oriental system' or *doctrina orientalis*" that would bind together Buddhism, Brahmanism, and Mesopotamian and Egyptian religions, along with the ideas of Pythagoras and Plato.[12] These examples, he suggests, demonstrate that the construction of a comparatist framework was founded on the belief in shared origins.

We might then think of this early Orientalist dream as being reincarnated, by the nineteenth century, as Blavatsky's notion of an "Oriental Cabala" (which she also spells in *Isis Unveiled* or elsewhere as "Kabala"): the esoteric doctrine that she said was available only to initiated "Adepts," and acted as "the great Oriental mother-root" of belief systems and traditions around the world.[13] In a letter published in *Spiritual Scientist* in September, 1875 – the same month that she cofounded the Theosophical Society with Col. Henry Steele Olcott, an American who was to be her closest collaborator – Blavatsky articulated her preference for personal experience and gnosis over scholarship. She also identified the Orient as the home of ultimate truth.

> One single journey to the Orient, made in the proper spirit . . . may quite as likely as not throw wide open to the zealous student, the heretofore closed doors of the final mysteries . . . . I will go further and say that such a journey,

---

[10] App, *Birth*, p. xi.    [11] App, *Birth*, p. 2.    [12] App, *Birth*, p. 4.
[13] Blavatsky, "Few Questions," p. 218.

performed with the omnipotent idea of one object, and with the help of a fervent will, is sure to produce more rapid, better, and more practical results, than the most diligent study of occultism in books – even though one were to devote to it dozens of years.[14]

As historians of the movement have written, Theosophy's embrace of India as the homeland of esoteric wisdom did not emerge in the Society's earliest years, and the location of this "Orient" was unclear. Even so, the article demonstrates that Blavatsky's own personal Orientalist affinities were already in place. Reading this, it is also evident that Blavatsky championed, from the earliest days of the Theosophical Society, a knowledge gleaned through initiation rather than book learning. At this relatively early moment, that pointed suggestion is turned against occultist texts, but within the next couple of years, she would mobilize it against Orientalist scholarship, while arguing that Theosophy's access to teachings far exceeded the reach of academic Orientalists.

It is telling that Blavatsky articulated these views in the spiritualist press. While Theosophical Orientalism might have embodied and extended certain preexisting strains within earlier writings on language and religion, it cannot be understood without reference to the milieu from which it emerged, as a product of the Victorian craze for occultism and spiritualism. Blavatsky herself allies the Oriental Kabala with the "the science of Occultism" that she describes as having given "birth to a variety of doctrines and various brotherhoods": in other words, a modern movement rooted in its own historical context. Despite Blavatsky's frequent assertions that the world's belief systems originated in the Orient, Theosophy was not as yet so clearly allied with specifically Indic traditions as it would grow to be; if anything, Blavatsky's allusions to the "Orient" or to "Oriental" mysteries could at times have alluded to Egypt, in keeping with the practices and preoccupations of contemporary Western occultism. Indeed, the name of the Society originally almost included "Rosicrucian" or "Hermetic" rather than "Theosophical," and either of the two titles would have specified a more clearly situated Western occultism than the rather abstract adjective that was ultimately chosen.[15] The literal meaning of "theosophy" (divine wisdom) refers to the philosophical belief that people have access to the divine within themselves: within the Western tradition, as Antoine Faivre writes, theosophy refers most generally to all perennialist attempts to compile this wisdom. After

---

[14] Blavatsky, "From Madame Blavatsky," p. 133.

[15] S. B. Liljegren describes this in *Bulwer-Lytton and Isis Unveiled*: The choice of "Theosophical" came after consulting a dictionary. Liljegren presents this as evidence that Blavatsky was taken with the Egyptian references in Bulwer-Lytton's work: One of the other possible names was "Egyptological" (Liljegren, *Bulwer-Lytton*, p. 11).

the seventeenth century, it specifically designated the body of thought shaped by Jacob Böhme. In the late nineteenth century, the term came to be associated with the Society's own syncretic philosophy.

Particularly in its earliest years, before Blavatsky and Olcott shifted headquarters (moving to India in 1879, and ultimately setting up their permanent headquarters in Adyar in 1882), the Theosophical Society sought to distill many disparate traditions – Boehmian theosophy, Kabbalah, Egyptology, Buddhism, and Vedanta – and vividly embodied this spectral infusion in a movement that was public, performative, and vociferously engaged with the cultural politics of its time, emerging as it did out of Victorian spiritualism. The late nineteenth century might be said to have witnessed a new avatar of esotericism through organizations like the Theosophical Society, the Hermetic Order of the Golden Dawn, the Societas Rosicruciana in Anglia, and the Swedenborgian Rite of Freemasonry (to name but a representative smattering of such societies), all of which sought to compile the theory and philosophies of occultist phenomena.[16] However arcane its references and however complex its esoteric doctrines, therefore, Theosophy emerged alongside other, similar bodies, in what Hugh Urban describes as the "teeming spiritual marketplace" of the nineteenth century, in which religion itself had become a "commodity"[17] – a time when, as Gauri Viswanathan describes it, "occultism had become the favorite sport of Britain's leisured classes."[18] Blavatsky and Olcott came together courtesy of this occultist craze, at a farmhouse in Vermont in 1875 where they went to witness spiritualist phenomena; later, their decision to start an organization came about, tellingly, soon after they attended a talk on "The Lost Canon of Proportion of the Egyptians."[19] In her writings, Blavatsky often presents these *au courant* interests as the modern and scientific aspects of Theosophy, all while she reaches back to the notion of an ancient, perennial wisdom.

## 2.1 Fiction, Fact, and Fantasy

A representative product (and popular commodity) within this new and buzzing occultist "marketplace" was *The Coming Race*, an early work of science fiction by Edward Bulwer-Lytton (sometime Secretary of State for the Colonies) that found a wide readership at the time, and clearly inspired Blavatsky – to the extent that she references the work several times in her first major work, *Isis*

---

[16] *The Theosophical Enlightenment*, by Joscelyn Godwin, surveys the different occultist organizations that emerged in the eighteenth and nineteenth centuries (somewhat from the perspective of a believer).

[17] Urban, *Secrecy*, p. 52.   [18] Viswanathan, "Ordinary Business," p. 1.

[19] Col. Olcott describes the making of this decision in the eighth chapter of his memoir, *Old Diary Leaves*.

*Unveiled* (1877), albeit as visionary document rather than fictional text. To read it closely allows us to see ways in which occultism and Orientalism came together as part of a broader quest for alternative cultural frameworks in Victorian Britain, though in a highly imaginative setting. The novella reflects Bulwer-Lytton's own interest in the occult, as it imagines a race of beings with mysterious powers beyond human capacity. Like Alice, its fictional narrator falls through a hole and into an adventure, when an inquisitive foray down a mineshaft lands him in the midst of an unknown subterranean civilization. At first, the narrator of *The Coming Race* finds uncanny resonances in this new world: The vegetation is unfamiliar but analogous to plants he knows, and the first gigantic building he encounters, which appears Egyptian from the outside, is "fitted up with an Oriental splendour" within.[20] The creatures of this skyless universe prove, too, to be at once alien and familiar. They are human, and yet "a type of man distinct from our known extant races":[21] red-skinned, dark-eyed, enormous, vaguely terrifying creatures fitted up with wings, and "with all the gravity and quietude of Orientals."[22] Moreover, the main source of their power is "vril," a form of "atmospheric magnetism" that powers not just the Vril-ya's wings, or their weaponry, locomotive transport, and physical illumination but also clairvoyance and telepathy. To a reading public caught up in the spiritualist craze, the idea would have been quite familiar: Bulwer-Lytton completes the likeness by explaining vril in the occultist terms of the 1850s and 1860s ("mesmerism, electro-biology, odic force, &c").[23]

Despite its otherworldly and fantastical setting, *The Coming Race* manifests a veridic impetus as well. This goes beyond the familiarity of its occultist terms. The narrator's repeated early references to the Vril-ya's "Oriental" qualities explicitly associate the powerful opacity of the fictional alien civilization with contemporary cultural encounters: As with many imperial fictions, for example, a prominently placed thwarted romance stages the impossibility of racial and ethnic mixing. Revealingly, the novella allegorizes these pervasive cultural anxieties as it relocates them to the otherworld of its speculative fiction. However, what is even more telling, for our purposes, is the way in which their expression draws in key textual referents. What makes *The Coming Race* so emblematic of its times, in other words, is the fluency with which its racial, sexual, and political preoccupations carom between – on the one side – the fantasies of Victorian occultism, and – on the other – the

---

[20] Bulwer-Lytton, *Coming Race*, p. 41. Notably, Bulwer-Lytton's conflation of the Egyptian and Oriental would go on to influence Blavatsky, such as when she discusses the "Oriental Kabala " in *Isis Unveiled*, a text named after an Egyptian goddess.

[21] Bulwer-Lytton, *Coming Race*, p. 20.      [22] Bulwer-Lytton, *Coming Race*, p. 24.

[23] Bulwer-Lytton, *Coming Race*, p. 20.

taxonomical impulses of Orientalist scholarship, which find frequent echoes in the anthropological conceit of the narrative.

One of the most intriguing aspects of Bulwer-Lytton's novel might well be the legend on its frontispiece: *The Coming Race* is "Inscribed to Max Müller in tribute of respect and admiration."[24] The eminent Indologist seems worlds away from an occultist novel about subterranean beings; and yet, by the twelfth chapter, he has climbed off the dedication page and into the novel.

> One of the most illustrious of recent philologists, Max Müller, in arguing for the analogy between the strata of language and the strata of the earth, lays down this absolute dogma: "No language can, by any possibility, be inflectional without having passed through the agglutinative and isolating stratum. No language can be agglutinative without clinging with its roots to the underlying stratum of isolation."

The sentence concludes by assiduously citing its source: "*'On the Stratification of Language' p. 20.*"[25]

By quoting Friedrich Max Müller's analogy between geological strata and morphological linguistic evolution, Bulwer-Lytton introduces a metaphor that clearly encompasses the central conceit of his novella: that of distinct civilizations and languages, layered above and below ground. The specific ideas that the narrator cites from Müller, however, barely address this basic applicability. Instead, they serve to structure his own pseudo-philology of the fictional Vril-ya language. In the remainder of that particular chapter, the narrator uses Müller's philological classifications to concoct an evolutionary account of this mysterious language (complete with explanatory examples and grammatical details). Thus, like languages from the "Turanian" family – and here, Bulwer-Lytton is explicitly borrowing from Müller's ill-fated proposal of a Central Asian language family of that name – the earliest forms of the Vril-ya language featured isolated, monosyllabic roots; thereafter, the language was "agglutinative," in that different roots were added to each other; and finally, the Vril-ya now have an "inflectional" language. As such, we are told, the singular of "An," or man, becomes pluralized as "Ana"; in full pseudo-philologist mode, the narrator explains that the letter "Na," as likened to "the Aryan root Nak, expressive of perishing or destruction," adds a negative connotation to words, while "Gy" and "An" for female and male, of course, recall their Greek roots.[26] Throughout, the chapter refers to familiar philological benchmarks.

Bulwer-Lytton's references to Max Müller seem to anchor his occultist fiction in a foundation of philological fact, but that grounding discourse has

---

[24] Bulwer-Lytton, *Coming Race*, p. 5.    [25] Bulwer-Lytton, *Coming Race*, p. 71.
[26] Bulwer-Lytton, *Coming Race*, pp. 72–73.

its own relationship with fantasy. "On the Stratification of Languages," which Müller delivered at Cambridge University in 1868, represents one station in his long campaign to define classificatory principles for the discipline of philology. As the novel suggests, the talk argues for a disciplinary correspondence between geology and philology, by establishing a correspondence between the evolutionary strata of the earth and the evolutionary strata of languages. However, the exact points at which Müller articulates this correspondence sound like nothing so much as the basic premise of *The Coming Race*. His paper begins by considering the role of wonder in the formation of a science. Müller imagines generations of humanity who remained incurious about the layers of the earth and, thus, ignorant of its science: "for thousands of years they must have seen in their quarries and mines, as well as we ourselves, the imbedded petrifactions of organic creatures: yet they looked and passed on without thinking more about it – they did not wonder."[27] In *The Coming Race*, Bulwer-Lytton's protagonist, who looks, wonders, enters the mine, and falls through to encounter the creatures of the Vril-ya world, is no more than a narrative enactment of Müller's rhetorical trope. Similarly, the novel's stratification of languages below and above ground offers a literal performance of Müller's analogy between philology and geology, which rests on the idea that certain "primitive" languages such as Chinese fossilize the historical traces of linguistic evolution – again, the philological conjecture reveals its own imprinting by contemporary Darwinism.

By the end of the novel, the metaphor of different strata that obtrude onto one another through evolutionary change figures as a fear that the "Coming Race" will rise from its subterranean incubus to overwhelm modern civilization through its superior knowledge and powers. Like the novel as a whole, the philological twelfth chapter ends with the fantasy of a record that will survive the narrator's death, as if to suggest that the novelistic and philological exercise together constitute a bulwark against destruction at the hands of an alien civilization, or at the very least, a talisman that will outlast the obliterating effects of this inevitable destruction: "Should life be spared to me, I may collect into systematic form such knowledge as I acquired of this language …. But what I have already said will perhaps suffice to show to genuine philological students that [this] language … must have been the gradual work of countless ages and many varieties of mind."[28]

There is much in *The Coming Race* to suggest that the arcane academic talk for "genuine philological students" is in concord with the high pitch of anxiety that also emanates from the novel. In his last few pages, the narrator concludes

---

[27] Müller, "Stratification," p. 64.   [28] Bulwer-Lytton, *Coming Race*, p. 77.

that while the Vril-ya were "originally not only of our human race, but, as seems to me clear by the roots of their language, descended from the same ancestors as the great Aryan family, from which in varied streams has flowed the dominant civilisation of the world," they are now "a distinct species" that will emerge above ground only to "destroy and replace our existing varieties of man."[29]

## 2.2 Aryan Family Values

*The Coming Race*'s description of the Vril-ya, as at once related (through a shared "great Aryan" ancestry that makes itself known through etymological evidence) and alien to "our existing varieties of man," brings together the imaginary beings of occultist science fiction and the preoccupations of contemporary Orientalists. Its specification of the Vril-ya's ancestry situates the warning of the novella's last few pages squarely within the broader philological discourse that linked the languages and races of Europe to those of the Orient. By the late nineteenth century, the term "Aryan" was the common term for the Indo-European language family, and had also taken on the racial overtones implied by Bulwer-Lytton's reference to "the dominant civilisation of the world."[30] In voicing his apprehensions about a civilization that is at once highly developed, alien, and related to his own, the gloomy protagonist of *The Coming Race* is bringing into narrative form a fairly widespread phantasmal relation. As European scholars of the eighteenth and nineteenth centuries researched the religions, languages, literatures, and histories of lands that had become newly accessible through imperial exploration and conquest (such as India, Egypt, Persia, and Turkey), the notion of a genealogical link enabled colliding conjectures even as it became widely accepted: that these cultures had degenerated into their current state from a glorious, shared ancestry; that they represented an earlier stage in the evolution of the Aryan people than the Europeans; and finally, that they had preserved the original language and religion of the Aryans more faithfully than the changeful societies of the West.[31] In other words, the trails of etymology seem to lead back not only to the protolanguage but also to the notion of an original community that once shared a system of

---

[29] Bulwer-Lytton, *Coming Race*, pp. 158–159.

[30] The novel participates in the rhetoric of race science in other, noteworthy ways: through its frequent asides about the "*mésalliance*" of interracial couplings such as "intermarriage between the Anglo-Saxon emigrants and the Red Indians" (Bulwer-Lytton, *Coming Race*, p. 159), and also through a sustained phrenological discussion of skull types, pigmentation and so on (Bulwer-Lytton, *Coming Race*, pp. 86–87).

[31] For a broader overview of the history of the Aryan hypothesis, particularly in the context of India, see Romila Thapar's "Reflections on Looking Again at the Aryan Question." See also Bryant, *Quest*.

beliefs as well as basic social structures.[32] In relocating the cathectic work of philology and ethnology within an otherworldly fantasy, *The Coming Race* takes such conjectures to an imaginative extreme, oriented (as its title suggests) around the future. For the amateur philologist who narrates the novel, the Vril-ya are threatening, ultimately, because they have moved on from the kinship of shared origins to an alien racial and cultural identity – and because the awe-inspiring powers and knowledge they amass, in the process, promise the destruction of "our civilization."[33] The fearful desires generated around racial difference and cultural kinship are plain to see in this occultist–Orientalist allegory, with its vivid vision of possible annihilation at the hands of beings who are at once related to and estranged from British culture. As such, the novella testifies to the uncanny intensities generated by seemingly dry scholarly hypotheses.

It is strikingly apparent, too, that *The Coming Race* takes for granted its readers' familiarity with the notion of the Aryan family. The assumed obvious-ness of a common kinship invites us to open the close reading of this occultist novella out into a wider historical narrative. The ease with which Bulwer-Lytton allows the terminology of agglutinative roots and Aryan families into his fantastical fiction suggests the significance of comparative philology at this time – not unlike finding the preoccupations of comparative religion reflected in Mr. Casaubon's quest for the Key to all Mythologies in *Middlemarch,* or those of ethnology in the arcane passions of Colonel Creighton or Hurree Babu in *Kim,* but more central to the very conception of the literary work in question. We turn then from Bulwer-Lytton to the broader history out of which his work grew – which he draws explicitly into its fiction, as we have noted, through the network of references. To consider this broader history, we will undertake a brief archaeology of the notion of linguistic kinship that grew into the conception of the Aryan family, first in philological and then ethnological and racial terms. These, as we will go on to examine, find their own echoes and reflections in the arcane cosmologies of Blavatsky's Theosophical writings.

In the late eighteenth century, William Jones was the most prominent (though not, strictly, the first) source of the hypothesis of the Indo-European language family. In 1786, Jones famously argued for a linguistic relationship between Sanskrit, Greek, Latin, Persian, and a select few other languages, in his "Third

---

[32] Ronald Inden, for instance, cites the distinguished Oxford Sanskritist and contemporary of Müller, Monier Monier-Williams, as responding in 1894 to a query about Vedic deities that "these were probably the very deities worshipped under similar names by our Aryan progenitors in their primeval home somewhere on the table-land of Central Asia" (quoted in Inden, *Imagining India*, p. 99).

[33] Bulwer-Lytton, *Coming Race*, p. 168.

Anniversary Discourse" before the Asiatic Society of Bengal in Calcutta. While Jones marveled that Sanskrit was "more perfect than the *Greek*, more copious than the *Latin*,"[34] he did not go so far as to dub it the source of Greek and Latin: instead, he hypothesized that these languages were themselves descended from another, original language (a hypothesis that has remained, positing a lost original language we now call proto-Indo-European).[35] In the decades following this epiphanic moment, evidence of this earlier kinship would feed into an Indomania that galvanized Europe, particularly Germany, during the heights of Romanticism. Friedrich Schlegel, for instance, wrote to a friend in 1803 that "*everything*, everything, originated in India without exception."[36]

As foundational twentieth-century historians of language and race like Léon Poliakov, Maurice Olender, and Thomas Trautmann have remarked, Jones's conclusion after studying Sanskrit, Latin, and Greek – that they must all have "sprung from some common source" – folded a search for the original language of Eden, one that stretched as far back as the medieval and early modern periods, into a new theory.[37] During the early years of the discipline of comparative philology, the taxonomies of language were still indebted to the Biblical story of Noah, Shem, Ham, and Japhet, and for that reason the Indo-European languages were also called "Japhetic." German scholars went on to use "Indo-Germanic" rather than "Indo-European," a phrase that Thomas Young coined in 1813.[38] The term "Aryan" first appears in the works of eighteenth-century Orientalists like Abraham-Hyacinthe Anquetil-Duperron and Jones himself, arising from the fact that it was a word with some currency in three separate streams of the Indo-European family of languages: namely, Persian, Sanskrit, and Greek.[39] "Aryan" gained some traction through Schlegel's usage, but ultimately Max Müller was responsible for its widespread adoption in English during the nineteenth century, as the primary name for the family of languages.[40] Even as the Biblical "Japhetic" gave way to "Aryan," the new classification retained a racial-linguistic connotation that anticipated its

---

34  Jones, "Third Anniversary Discourse," p. 34.     35  Jones, "Third Anniversary Discourse."

36  Quoted in Germana, "Self-Othering." In the essay, Germana suggests that Schlegel believed modern-day Germans to be descended from India, and that Germany constituted an "Orient" within Europe.

37  Trautmann, *Aryans and British India*, p. 38.

38  For a useful history of the Indo-European hypothesis, as well as an overview of the relation between the "Mosaic ethnography" and the emerging ideas of early philology, see the first chapter of Arvidsson, *Aryan Idols*. A longer account of the European idea of India as a source of wisdom traditions lies outside the purview of this Element; the Indomania we examine here is inextricable from the broader, eighteenth- and nineteenth-century context of Romantic Orientalism. However, there is a case to be made for tracing it back to antiquity, at least as far back as Plotinus.

39  Arvidsson, *Aryan Idols*, p. 20.

40  See Arvidsson, *Aryan Idols*, p. 21, and Wiedemann, "The Aryans," p. 36.

eventual segue from a linguistic to a racial category, ultimately finding its genocidal apogee under Nazism in the twentieth century.[41] Overall, nineteenth-century conceptions of languages and races saw them as coextensive modes of kinship.[42]

If the founding moment of comparative philology incorporated the Biblical idea that all languages emerged from one divinely ordained language, the idea of a singular Edenic language whose decipherment might once more unlock the secrets of religion was the basis, too, of esoteric thought as signified by the Christian and Jewish Kabbalah. Before the philological hypotheses of the late eighteenth century, Hebrew had the strongest claim on being the original language of the Tower of Babel myth, but in the first flush of Romantic Orientalism, philologists speculated that Sanskrit itself might be this mysterious *Ur-Sprache*.[43] In their crucial writings on the Aryan hypothesis, Poliakov and Olender present convincing explications of the cultural fantasies invested in the Indo-European hypothesis. As Poliakov suggests, the idea of an Indo-European family located in India opened up the possibility of an alternative lineage for Christianity: a genealogy that had nothing to do with a Semitic identity. He quotes Arthur Schopenhauer as writing, for instance, that "Christian doctrine issuing from the wisdom of India has covered over the old trunk of gross Judaism."[44] While the full racial implications of this genealogy would become obvious only later in the nineteenth century (through the works of writers such as Arthur de Gobineau and Ernest Renan), Olender and Poliakov argue that

---

[41] There are several clear examples of biological, linguistic, and religious categories collapsing into the category of the "Aryan," even as early as the mid-nineteenth century. Poliakov writes that, according to Gobineau, the Aryans *were* the sons of Japheth: He combined Biblical descriptions of race with contemporary biological and linguistic narratives. Thus, while the sons of Noah – Ham, Shem, and Japheth – were all white, Gobineau explained that they had mixed with other races to produce degenerate "alloys," until all the bloodstreams of Europe were contaminated – only the Aryans, sons of Japheth, retained some pure white, although there were fewer and fewer pure Aryans. In 1856, he wrote: "The white species will disappear henceforth from the face of the earth . . .. The portion of Aryan blood, already subdivided so frequently, which still exists in our countries and which alone sustains the edifice of our society, advances daily towards the last frontier before total absorption" (Poliakov, *Aryan Myth*, p. 237).

[42] Wiedemann, "The Aryans," p. 33.

[43] Trautmann, *Aryans and British India*, p. 38. For the hold of "Indomania," particularly on German Orientalists like Johann Gottfried Herder, Friedrich Schlegel, and others, see Stefan Arvidsson, *Aryan Idols*, pp. 24–31. As Arvidsson writes, comparative philology's fascination with a common origin in the nineteenth century reflects the fact that "the genetic model of explanation became one of the basic building blocks of humanistic thinking in general: a phenomenon was not thoroughly illuminated until its origin was mapped out. This romantic search for origins was rarely a purely scientific theoretical postulate: it usually also had nostalgic undertones and was linked to a religious notion of origin as a state of unspoiled harmony" (Arvidsson, *Aryan Idols*, p. 27).

[44] Poliakov, *Aryan Myth*, p. 247. Similarly, Poliakov quotes Goethe as saying that his study of Zoroastrianism was motivated by a desire to escape "the narrow circle of Hebraic-Rabbinic thought and [reach] the depth and amplitude of Sanskrit" (Poliakov, *Aryan Myth*, p. 195).

the esoteric sub-text of philology – the search for a protolanguage that would conform to religious narratives – meant that the Biblical conflation of language and race was already a part of philological classifications. Since the early engine of comparative philology was etymology, as Stefan Arvidsson points out, it kept religion and language, too, contiguous with one another – for instance, through William Jones's momentous suggestion that the Roman "Jupiter" was etymologically related to "the Vedic Dyáuṣ pitā."[45] The obvious implication here is that the same shared ancestors who once all spoke the same protolanguage must also have worshipped the same deity. Religion, language, and race come together inextricably in ideas such as this; in their entanglement, we can discern new channels for the further growth of an esotericist belief in a mysterious perennial philosophy that was originally shared across now diverse wisdom traditions, in ways that we go on to explore.

Over the course of the nineteenth century, we see the philological focus on roots and etymological cognates increasingly give way to the rhetoric of biology, as newer formations like ethnology, Darwinism, and race science come to bear on the Aryan question.[46] By the mid-nineteenth century, for example, Gobineau was already describing Aryans as the most superior specimens of the white race.[47] The growing prevalence of such an attitude offered a kind of contestation and rebuttal of philology's earlier celebration of an original kinship. Instead, a turn to the investigative innovations of race science (such as craniology) emphasized biological differences between the Asian and European members of the Indo-European family, and fed new theories, such as the idea that an original race of white Aryans had invaded India and reshaped its language and religion, or the suggestion that it would be incorrect to group Asian and European Aryans as a family, rather than as colonized and colonizer.[48]

In the philological response to this development, we can see both vociferous objection and unwitting complicity. Müller, for instance, worked hard to distance his classification of Indo-European languages as Aryan from biological

---

[45] Trautmann, *Aryans and British India*, p. 38.

[46] One of the foundational books to describe the enthusiasms of Romantic Orientalism and trace the shifts that took place across the nineteenth century is Raymond Schwab's influential account in *The Oriental Renaissance*.

[47] Wiedemann, "The Aryans," p. 42.

[48] Trautmann cites Isaac Taylor as arguing, in 1889, that the original white Aryans invaded India, conquered the dark aboriginals who lived there (and thus established the caste system), "but the purity of the race was soiled by marriage with native women, the language was infected with peculiar Dravidian sounds, and the creed with foul Dravidian worships of Siva and Kali, and the adoration of the lingam and the snake" (Trautmann, *Aryans and British India*, p. 185). Note that Taylor's discussion of how the "race" was "soiled" takes in biology, language, religion, and sexuality, as well as absorbing the logic of caste.

taxonomies, writing that "[t]here are Aryan and Semitic languages, but it is against all rules of logic to speak, without an expressed or implied qualification, of an Aryan race, of Aryan blood, of Aryan skulls … many misunderstandings, many controversies, would have been avoided, if scholars had not attempted to draw conclusions from language to blood, or from blood to language."[49] Such an emphasis on languages also allows Müller to avoid the other leaps implied by this facile jump "from language to blood," such as a matching swerve from language to creed or from creed to blood. In an 1860 review entitled "Semitic Monotheism," he quotes Ernest Renan as saying that the Semitic races were "monotheistic in religion, lyrical in poetry, monarchical in politics, abrupt in style, and useless for speculation."[50] Müller took particular exception to Renan's identification of monotheism as an "instinct" of the Semitic races, explaining instead that the differences were in fact purely linguistic: The roots of words in Semitic languages remain obvious, whereas in Aryan languages, the prefixes and suffixes and various morphologies of the words obscure the original root of the word entirely. That is why, he tells us, Aryan languages include various metaphorical and mythological names for God, whereas in Semitic languages such plurality is restricted to adjectives, while the root remains constant. For Müller, all religions strive toward one monistic divinity: Polytheism and monotheism are simply linguistic variations that communicate the same singular spiritual apprehension. In its own way, this harkening back to a singular core shared across religions is a theosophical impulse, reminiscent of the early modern affinity for esotericism and self-discovery that App presents as a constitutive element of the early Orientalist interest in Asian religions.

However, despite this strong denunciation, philology is not entirely free of the tendency to see blood, creed, and tongue as coextensive.[51] Müller's position entails a strong denunciation of race science's appropriation of linguistic genealogies and families – and yet, there are times when those presiding conceits of genealogy and family, even if applied to the history of languages, make such a crisscrossing seem almost unavoidable. In the very same talk in which he rejects the notion of "Aryan blood" and "Aryan skulls," he makes precisely such a move himself, while metaphorically revisiting the original

---

[49] Müller, *Chips Vol. 4*, p. 211.

[50] Müller, *Chips Vol. 1*, p. 339. Müller explains that "Semitic" used to just mean Jews and Arabs, but now it includes the three religions of Judaism, Islam, and Christianity; moreover, he cites Renan as distinguishing between "the nomad branch" of the family ("Arabs, Hebrews," and Palestinians) and "the political branch" ("the nations of Phenicia, of Syria, Mesopotamia, and Yemen") (Müller, *Chips Vol. 1*, p. 340).

[51] The disciplinary history of religious studies going back to the seventeenth and eighteenth centuries may also have contributed to the taxonomical, comparative instincts that show up in philology and comparative religion. See Hunt, Jacob, and Mijnhardt, *The Book that Changed Europe*, as well as Muslow, "Antiquarianism and Idolatry."

Aryan family: "even in these faint pulsations of language, in the changes of accent in Greek and Sanskrit, may we feel the common blood that runs in the vein of the old Aryan dialects."[52] This inability to keep systems of language and biology apart in his figures of thought, in the evocation of "common blood," is indicative of conflations within the larger comparative project. Ultimately, the philological opposition to race science keeps getting ensnared in its own previous assumptions about the coextensive nature of language and race. Looking back, it is possible to see that the biologism of late-nineteenth-century understandings of race simply repurposed this already existent confusion of tongues, creeds, and peoples, but ordered them into a hierarchical classification that rejected the promise of kinship in favor of othering and disavowal.

## 3 Theosophical Orientalism

As we will go on to see, the contemporary ethnological preoccupations with race and bloodlines, Aryans and Semites, made their way into even the recondite texts of Theosophy. What makes Blavatsky's works so fascinating for our purposes, however, is their incoherence around these matters. On the one hand, she draws from contemporary philology and ethnology in enacting her own entanglements of race, language, and religion; on the other, she presciently critiques the attitudes of racial superiority that undergird "exoteric" Western approaches to Oriental "wisdom traditions." Instead, Blavatsky's writings consistently and vociferously advocate the idea that only practitioners and "initiates" know the real meaning of sacred texts – arcane truths that must be sourced through direct teaching, rather than being simply decoded via acts of expert translation. Even as this fundamental axiom redirects the authority to interpret and explain texts away from Western Orientalism toward India and Tibet,

---

[52] Müller, *Chips Vol. 4*, p. 211. Müller's work often does have colliding strains within it when it comes to the vexed relation between language and race. Such contradictions can be explained, to an extent, by the fact that during the 1850s, he extended the classification of a language family to actual people and families, imagining the Aryan protolanguage being spoken by "a small family living under one and the same roof" (Müller, *Chips Vol. 2*, p. 19) – only to recant in 1872, when the most inimical implications of that conflation were already taking shape. But even thereafter, as in this 1874 address to the International Congress of Orientalists, he returns to the metaphor of an actual family of people as much as of languages: "[T]he curtain between the West and the East has been lifted, and our old forgotten home stands before us again in bright colours and definite outlines. Two worlds, separated for thousands of years, have been reunited as by a magic spell, and we feel rich in a past that may well be the pride of our noble Aryan family" (Müller, *Chips Vol. 4*, p. 325). And yet, desirous as this vision seems, Müller's disgust at the appropriation of philological terms for racist taxonomies is palpable in "The Home of the Aryas": "To me an ethnologist who speaks of Aryan race, Aryan blood, Aryan eyes and hair, is as great a sinner as a linguist who speaks of a dolichocephalic dictionary or a brachycephalic grammar. It is worse than a Babylonian confusion of tongues – it is downright theft. We have made our own terminology for the classification of languages; let ethnologists make their own for the classification of skulls, and hair, and blood" (Müller, "The Home of the Aryas," pp. 120–121).

however, the content of the perennial wisdom or the Oriental Kabala is by no means a radically unfamiliar epistemology. As we will go on to discuss, the "secret doctrine," which Blavatsky describes as the ancient wisdom passed on to her by Theosophy's Masters, is rife with the contemporary Orientalist discourse of the Aryan family, and frequently echoes and extends the contemporary Western discourse of race and caste.

Before entering into the content of these writings, and the way in which they engage philology and ethnology, it is important to locate them in a historical narrative by tracing the broader outlines of Theosophical Orientalism. While Blavatsky, as we have seen, championed the wisdom of the East from the earliest days of the Theosophical Society, the unspecified "Orient" of these earlier writings became increasingly anchored in Indic traditions like Vedanta and Buddhism over time, particularly after the Society's cofounders shifted to India in 1879.[53] In its earliest years, the Theosophical Society's aims were in keeping with the broader preoccupations of the spiritualist movement, with the addition of a kind of syncretic idealism that had also inspired Orientalists like Max Müller. In Olcott's summary of the Society's mission in 1878, Theosophy was originally motivated by "the aspiration for the attainment of spiritual knowledge through the study of natural, especially of occult, phenomena ... as well as the brotherhood of mankind."[54] In 1886, Blavatsky wrote "the Original Programme of the Theosophical Society," which explained that her mysterious Masters (or Mahatmas) in Tibet had overseen the founding of the Society in order to fulfill – as in Olcott's summary – the ideal of "Universal Brotherhood," and to oppose distinctions based on "races, creeds or social positions"; as before, she explained that the organization had come into being to challenge materialism and religious dogma; but perhaps most significantly, Theosophists were also now said to have been always motivated to "study the philosophies of the East – those of India chiefly, presenting them gradually to the public in various works that would interpret exoteric religions in the light of esoteric teachings."[55]

---

[53] Apart from Olcott's account of these early years in India in *Old Diary Leaves,* we can turn to A. P. Sinnett's eyewitness discussion of Blavatsky and Olcott's first travels in India in Sinnett, *Incidents of the Life of Madame Blavatsky.*

[54] Olcott, *Old Diary Leaves*, p. 399. Olcott's descriptions of the 1878 mission statement comes in a chapter devoted to Theosophy's schism with "Swami Dyánand" and the Arya Samaj: Olcott compares the Arya Samaj objectives to those of Theosophy in order to demonstrate that the Theosophical Society could not have remained in an alliance with the Samaj after realizing that it was primarily Hindu and thus a "sectarian body" (Olcott, *Old Diary Leaves,* p. 403). The Society's bylaws at the time of its founding (in 1875) state, simply, that "the objects of the society are, to collect and diffuse a knowledge of the laws which govern the universe" (Ransom, *Short History*, p. 545). Ransom's appendix on the "Objects and Rules of the Theosophical Society" is a useful record of the Society's changing self-definition. See Ransom, *Short History.*

[55] Blavatsky, *Original Programme*, pp. 1–2.

About two years after writing "The Original Programme," Blavatsky created an autonomous body within the Society called the Esoteric Section, setting forth its objects in a "Preliminary Memorandum." As the memorandum makes clear, its author was dissatisfied with the Society's focus on "Universal Brotherhood" at the expense of occultism, and heralded the Esoteric Section as a core study group that would revitalize the Society's esoteric objectives and thus the organization as a whole: "It is only by a select group of brave souls, a handful of determined men and women hungry for genuine spiritual development and the acquirement of soul-wisdom, that the Theosophical Society at large can be brought back to its original lines."[56] Since Olcott was apprehensive that the ES would become a "Jesuitical" nucleus within the Society, its name was changed, in Blavatsky's lifetime, to "the Eastern School of Theosophy": an instance of the facility with which "esoteric" and "Eastern" slip into each other in the narratives of Theosophy.

The various manifestos through which the Society defined itself thus register the shifts and revisions that marked its early history. The context for the 1886 restatement of the Society's mission in the "Original Programme" reveals that, increasingly, Theosophy defined its primary function as the performance of what Joy Dixon has called its "amateur Orientalism."[57] "The Original Programme" comes in the form of a defense against charges by two Theosophists, who seem to have criticized the Society for being too focused on its organization and bureaucracy. By way of passionate rebuttal, Blavatsky turns to the main achievement of the Society: "[W]ould Vedanta and other Hindu philosophies have been ever taught and studied in England outside the walls of Oxford and Cambridge, had it not been for that organization that fished them like forgotten pearls out of the Ocean of Oblivion and Ignorance and brought them forward before the profane world?"[58]

## 3.1 Major Works

As Blavatsky's rhetorical question makes clear, once it moved to India in 1879, Theosophy increasingly defined itself as a pedagogical alternative to Orientalist scholarship, even as it continued to lean on these philological sources. Müller – the best known Indologist within "the walls of Oxford" – is a frequent target, not only when she cites his claims on behalf of Indian culture but also when she attacks his scholarly methodology (although particularly her earlier writings do at times cite him and other Orientalists in more complimentary terms). In *Isis Unveiled,* for example, she scoffs at his

---

[56] Blavatsky, *Original Programme*, p. 67.    [57] Dixon, *Divine Feminine*, p. 43.
[58] Blavatsky, *Original Programme*, pp. 43–44.

inability to understand the true meaning of the Popol-Vuh, which Müller compared to the *Arabian Nights Entertainments*.

> Even the erudite and sober Max Müller is somehow unable to get rid of *coincidences*. To him they come in the shape of the most unexpected discoveries. . . . We think we can see how it is that Professor Müller confesses that "now and then . . . one imagine one sees certain periods and landmarks, but in the next page all is chaos again." May it not be barely possible that this chaos is intensified by the fact that most of the scientists, directing the whole of their attention to history, skip that which they treat as "vague, contradictory, miraculous, absurd."[59]

As the context of this passage makes clear, the kinds of *"coincidences"* to which Blavatsky refers are the motifs shared, inexplicably, by cultures not known to be historically linked, or claims of influence and transmission that Müller has dismissed for not meeting "scientific" criteria, and thus banished to the realm of the fantastical. One of the recurrent Theosophical criticisms of Orientalist scholarship centers on the imposition of exoteric, positivist structures of inquiry onto subjective, even supernatural, experiences of religion and culture; another, of course, concerns its textualist bias and neglect of interpretations from within the culture or religion under study.[60] Theosophy privileges the "vague, contradictory, miraculous, absurd" in service of a vision of ancient Oriental wisdom that could only be described (after Said) as genealogically related but "ontologically and epistemologically distinct" from the Occident. However, paradoxical as it might seem, Blavatsky's personal Orientalism enables a prescient deconstruction of the assumptions and axioms of academic Orientalism. Prefiguring Said by approximately a century, Blavatsky anticipates his specific critique of "flexible positional superiority" in Orientalist scholarship, as well as critiquing the unarticulated interdependence between Orientalist scholarship and empire. In *Isis Unveiled*, for instance, she writes of academic Orientalists that

> in most cases they do not even suspect that in the arcane philosophy of India there are depths which they have not sounded . . .. There is a pervading tone of conscious superiority, a ring of contempt in the treatment of Hindu metaphysics, as though the European mind is alone enlightened enough to polish the rough diamond of the old Sanscrit writers.[61]

---

[59] Blavatsky, *Isis Unveiled Vol. 1*, pp. 548–549.

[60] In this framing of a contest between "miraculous" and "absurd" wisdom on the one hand and textually authorized knowledge on the other, the controversies between Theosophists and Indologists are not unlike the discord between spiritualists and theologians in the same period. Like Blavatsky in this instance, spiritualists also claimed the authority of direct, personal experience, as well as their testimony of supernatural communication, against the scriptural authority of theologians.

[61] Blavatsky, *Isis Unveiled Vol. 2*, pp. 102–103.

At another point, she critiques scholarly collusion with Church and Empire, remarking sarcastically that "[o]f late there has been a touching accord between philologists holding high official positions, and missionaries from heathen lands."[62] The link that she draws between supposedly disinterested scholars and their participation in colonial administration clearly anticipates the Saidian critique of Orientalist scholarship and study as being inescapably bound to, and ultimately in service of, the imperial project.

Nonetheless, we see a growing engagement with Orientalist sources in the major Theosophical writings, particularly Blavatsky's two best-known works. *Isis Unveiled* and *The Secret Doctrine* both assert mastery over the "ancient wisdom" that, Blavatsky argues, was lost to Western culture with the spread of Christianity and scientism, but retained by mysterious adepts in (variously) Egypt, India, and Tibet. While *Isis Unveiled* seeks to demonstrate the superiority of the secret "Oriental Kabala" over exoteric science, religion, and academic Orientalism, *The Secret Doctrine* claims to actually unfold the content of the ancient wisdom in compiling a quasi-evolutionary theory of human and cosmic history, in which the motor of reincarnation transports planetary systems, life-forms, and human races through patterned phases.[63] Given the convolution of Blavatsky's schemata, I will now offer an overview of these major works, to better enable a discussion of their implications for the Theosophical approach to race and caste. I will also begin to enter more closely into the experience of reading Blavatsky, focusing on the contradictions, incoherences, and idiosyncrasies of her works – which help us read against the grain of academic Orientalism, and attest to the broader heterogeneity of the European discourse around "Eastern" religion and culture.

In *Isis Unveiled*, Blavatsky marshals a plethora of detail in service of clearly defined goals: to demonstrate, first, that all religions share their origins in a perennial philosophy far surpassing contemporary, exoteric philosophies and religions, and second, that this ancient wisdom was scientifically sophisticated enough to explain the supernatural phenomena now incomprehensible to modern science, being more closely allied to the concerns of Victorian occultism and spiritualism, such as the relationship among body, soul, and spirit.[64] As the name *Isis Unveiled* (with its reference to the Egyptian goddess) suggests, Blavatsky was

---

[62] Blavatsky, *Isis Unveiled Vol. 2*, p. 529.

[63] Julie Chajes remarks on the different approaches to reincarnation in the two texts, noting that while *Isis Unveiled* revolves around "metempsychosis," *The Secret Doctrine* is more concerned with reincarnation (Chajes, *Recycled Lives*, p. 4). Her monograph, *Recycled Lives*, attends to other significant distinctions between the two works while offering close readings of each.

[64] Chajes, *Recycled Lives*, p. 13. The précis of *Isis Unveiled* is based on Blavatsky, *Isis Unveiled, Vols. 1 & 2*. For my summary of *The Secret Doctrine*, I rely on Blavatsky, *The Secret Doctrine*. In making this brief summary, I also consulted the following works: Preston and Humphreys (eds.), *Abridgement*; Viswanathan, *Outside the Fold;* Risseeuw, "Thinking Culture through Counter-Culture"; Campbell, *Ancient Wisdom Revived*.

influenced by Egyptology while writing the book, and at times the "Oriental Kabala" Blavatsky writes about has an Egyptian cast.[65] Regardless of the cultural situation of the Kabala, however, it is firmly presented as a compendium of syncretic knowledge, and one that is posited against the assumptions and methods of philology. As the book continually argues, academic Orientalists are uninitiated into cultural knowledge, and are consequently unable to factor into their analyses and representations the esoteric interpretations and practices preserved by Oriental adepts. In Gauri Viswanathan's reading of Blavatsky, this "radical reorientation of method" allowed Blavatsky to assert the "continuing vitality" of beliefs that Orientalist scholarship would otherwise consign to a "frozen textual archive associated with an irretrievable past": it becomes the defining breach between academic Orientalism and Theosophy in this period, and allows for a lively contestation, despite the several and significant overlaps between these two versions of interdisciplinary, comparative, transcultural study.[66]

Within the text, the proper names that distinguish one race from another often come across as the detritus of a partial, exoteric historiography. At one point, for instance, Blavatsky explains that while the story of Genesis was derived from the Chaldeans and the Akkadians, she believes the Akkadians to be "cognate with the Brahmans, of Hindustan."[67] Given the nominality of racial categories in the text, this use of "cognate" seems almost intentionally punning in its simultaneous recall of bloodline and etymology. The elasticity of racial categories at so many places in *Isis Unveiled* appears strangely contrary to the determinism that characterizes them at other points, as when Blavatsky asserts that "[r]aces of men differ in spiritual gifts as in color, stature, or any other external quality," or even when she rails against Christian dogma. In fact, such contradictions so blatantly enact the fundamental illogic of racial taxonomies – at once hierarchical and recombinant – that they become allegories of that illogic.[68]

---

[65] This may have been influenced by Edward Bulwer-Lytton's conflation of "Egyptian" and "Oriental," for instance, in his 1834 novel, *The Last Days of Pompeii*. Even the unambiguously Western occultism of Bulwer-Lytton produced its own strange "Egyptian Orientalism," doubtless inspired by the late-eighteenth-century Orientalist wish to establish the interdependence of Egyptian, Indian, and Greek antiquities. Bulwer-Lytton's depiction of Egypt as the source of all occultism revisits the nineteenth-century Egyptological idea that all civilization arose in Egypt, which closely followed the Romantic belief that all civilization arose in India. Perhaps because of Liljegren's monograph, it is not uncommon to come across such overstatements as Nicholas Goodrick-Clark's: "It is ironical that early theosophy should have been principally inspired by English occult fiction" (Goodrick-Clark, *Occult Roots*, p. 18). In Theosophical texts, one frequently comes across references to Bulwer-Lytton: for instance, the fifth Mahatma letter to A. P. Sinnett mentions "Mejnoor" as an example of the relationship between initiate and "master" (a reference to Bulwer-Lytton's *Zanoni*); the same letter also discusses "vril" from Bulwer-Lytton's *The Coming Race*. See A. T. Barker (ed.), *The Mahatma Letters*, p. 32.

[66] Viswanathan, "In Search," pp. 83–84.    [67] Blavatsky, *Isis Unveiled Vol. 1*, p. 576.

[68] Blavatsky, *Isis Unveiled Vol. 2*, p. 588.

While extending this methodological unconventionality and continuing to offer a syncretic approach to the matter of Eastern wisdom, *The Secret Doctrine* seeks to incorporate even grander totalities than *Isis Unveiled*. When the book first came out, in 1888, it was divided into two volumes, "Cosmogenesis" and "Anthropogenesis," which together unfolded the narrative of universal and human evolution as per "the Secret Doctrine," the essence and source of all religions (in other words, homologous with *Isis Unveiled*'s "Oriental Kabala"). The text claims to compile, along with Blavatsky's own explicatory annotations, the translation of a mysterious epic poem written in the esoteric language of "Senzar" and made available to her by the Masters. In an introductory section, Blavatsky asserts that the secret doctrine is based on fundamental principles: there is a basic "Reality," out of which life emerges; the universe is based on periods and cycles; all souls are part of an oversoul and go through cycles of reincarnation. She also asserts that this doctrine is the content of the esoteric wisdom that lies concealed within the various exoteric traditions of Europe and the Orient. As the preface announces: "[W]hat is contained in this work is to be found scattered throughout thousands of volumes embodying the scriptures of the great Asiatic and early European religions, hidden under glyph and symbol, and hitherto left unnoticed because of this veil."[69]

Both *The Secret Doctrine* and *Isis Unveiled* seek to present themselves as scholarly inquiries into the comparative findings of mythology and religion, with the additional benefit of occult training from theosophical initiates that will allow the reader to penetrate this "veil." *The Secret Doctrine* is full of such moments, as when Blavatsky expounds upon the esoteric symbology that can conjure forth the real meaning of holy signs like the cross, or when she compares the "true" significance of the number seven in Hindu and Egyptian wisdom traditions. Like *Isis Unveiled*, the text engages contemporary science and cites the findings of "Esoteric Science" to argue against the evolutionary theories of Charles Darwin and Ernst Haeckel, even while adopting their methodological conventions and terminology – all while unfolding an elaborate cosmology.[70] Like many other esoteric cosmologies, this grand system traces the correspondences between cosmic, human, and natural orders, but

---

[69] Blavatsky, *Secret Doctrine Vol. 1*, p. i.

[70] As Frederick C. Crews' colorful description puts it, *The Secret Doctrine* reads "like a hashish-induced satire on *The Descent of Man*" (Crews, "Consolation," p. 27). In fact, Blavatsky was an enthusiastic consumer of hashish. As Wouter Hanegraaff puts it, while discussing a contemporary newspaper advertisement for "hasheesh" as an "Eastern remedy, Used for Thousands of Years by the Ancient Hindoos, Persians, Jews, Greeks, Chinese, Japanese, Arabians, Egyptians, Chaldeans and the Assyrians" (which sounds very much like Blavatsky's "ancient wisdom"): "given Blavatsky's basic interests, how indeed could she *not* have been interested in hashish?" (Hanegraaff, "Theosophical Imagination," p. 13).

along with Darwinian language, Blavatsky mobilizes timescales, cosmological rhythms, and untranslated Sanskrit terms from Hindu philosophy to do so. Thus, as in the Puranas, the universe (which is itself one among many universes) moves through various periods of Manvantara and Pralaya (evolution and dissolution), going through what Blavatsky describes as sevenfold evolutionary processes that mirror the sevenfold evolution of human races, with beings or "monads" who are reincarnated to move through these universal cycles.[71] Planets themselves have a septenary constitution, since each physical planet (including the earth) is accompanied by six "invisible" globes and undergoes a seven-stage evolutionary cycle in which it moves from a spiritual to physical to spiritual level, before beginning a new cycle. At the present juncture, *The Secret Doctrine* asserts, the earth is in its fourth round, that is, on its way back to a spiritual rather than physical existence.

In the second volume of the work, "Anthropogenesis," the earth's septenary evolution is shown to be mirrored by the evolution of human beings ("monads" that have been reincarnated several times on their way into human form), which takes them, too, through different rounds that are divided into seven successive "root races." These different races similarly represent various stages of a septenary cycle that moves from a spiritual to a physical and back to a spiritual plane of existence. In the context of human evolution, this cycle manifests through the transition from the disembodied, nonsexually reproducing beings of the first root race to people with blood, bones, and sexual differentiation, like those of the current (fifth, Aryan) root race, eventually reaching another level of purely spiritual existence, with the beginning of the next round of evolution. The various root races emerge sequentially from different geographical areas – the North Pole, Atlantis, Asia – and are shown to be distinct from one another through such varying traits as size, color, and means of reproduction, as well as differing intellectual and spiritual capacities. The subraces of the various root races are generally also recognizable, much like the category of "Aryan": for instance, the fifth subrace of the current root race is that of the "Anglo-Saxon."

## 3.2 Visions of Race

The apparent otherworldliness of *The Secret Doctrine*'s cosmology is, clearly, not much of a mask for its identification with the categories and assumptions

---

[71] Each Manvantara is as long as a "Day of Brahma," which lasts 4,320,000,000 years. A "Year of Brahma" has 360 such days in it, and 100 such years compose a "Maha-Kalpa" or great age, which in turn lasts 311,040,000,000,000 years. These terms and figures are more or less derived from Hindu religious and mythological texts like the Vishnu Puranas, demonstrating the scale of time that Blavatsky opposes to Biblical time (Preston and Humphreys, *Abridgment*, p. 19).

of contemporary ethnology and race science. The category of the Aryan is specified as a "root race," a term whose inaccessibility seemingly distinguishes it from the "race" we know through general usage: the idea that some root races propagated through asexual reproduction, for instance, approaches the terrain of science fiction (somewhat like the gigantic Vril-ya of *The Coming Race*, whose biological constitution is beyond the human). And yet, as critics including Isaac Lubelsky, James Santucci, and Carla Risseeuw have suggested, *The Secret Doctrine*'s abstracted use of the term still refracts nineteenth-century taxonomies, and bears the imprint of evolutionary thought. As Santucci points out, for instance, the notion of spiritual progress connecting various root races contributes to a hierarchy of inferior and superior races. Each root race has its own seven subraces: some of these signal the coming of a new root race; others are the vestiges of inappropriate pairings between different root races. These root races are classified and described according to a hyperbolically biological taxonomy: one race gives rise to another by "budding"; there are several references to (arguments against, appropriations of) natural selection; indeed, whole chapters seem devoted to esoteric challenges to Darwin and Haeckel. Unlike Müller's strong (if occasionally self-defeating) objection to the ethnological appropriation of the philological category of "Aryan," in Blavatsky's work we see the bricoleur's enthusiasm for adopting and making do with whatever discursive formation lies close at hand – including race science.

If anything, the evolutionary systems and classifications of *The Secret Doctrine* present an even more elaborate biological causality for the category of the Aryan than the racist works of a Gobineau or a Taylor.

> The evolution of these races, their formation and development, went *pari passu* and on parallel lines with the evolution, formation, and development of three geological strata, from which the human complexion was as much derived as it was determined by the climates …. The Aryan races, for instance, now varying from dark brown, almost black, red-brown-yellow, down to the whitest creamy color, are yet all of one and the same stock – the Fifth Root Race – and spring from one single Progenitor, called in Hindu *exotericism* by the generic name of Vaivasvata Manu.[72]

Blavatsky's theory of races unambiguously seeks a supernatural validation for classifications that had, in fact, emerged from nothing more eternal or transcendent than the racial assumptions of nineteenth-century ethnology. Her concept of race echoes its Victorian contemporaries, however, only to enmesh them in a wildly implausible system, offering no more than its own assertion of

---

[72] Blavatsky, *Secret Doctrine Vol. 2*, p. 223.

a link to connect the scientific jargon of geology and evolution to the exotic names of "Hindu *exotericism*."

*The Secret Doctrine* reformulates ethnology's speculative connections – between race and geographical origin, or race and evolution – with a vivid literalism: for example, the concept of phenotype is reincarnated, here, as a direct correlation between "geological strata" and "complexion." Given the reductive directness of these correspondences, it comes as a surprise to discover that the ironclad causal links of Blavatsky's system allow for a rich array of possible racial consequences: not only are Aryans not necessarily white, they are "dark brown, almost black, red-brown-yellow, down to the whitest creamy color." Like the proliferating nouns that supposedly describe ethnicity or culture in *Isis Unveiled* (but which seem to disperse categories of identity across a nominal mélange), this inventory of possible pigments denatures the very causality of race that it ostensibly catalogues. Instead, Blavatsky's Anthropogenesis becomes a parable about ethnology's construction of race as a natural category through the ascription of natural causes, the specification of traits, and the determination of an origin and a genealogy.[73]

Carla Risseuw has argued that "theosophy uses the concept of race, in a wider context than that of physical characteristics alone . . . these outer characteristics are unalterably linked to inner characteristics, merging exponents of each race to the civilization they create."[74] Even so, Theosophy transgresses the carefully narrow boundaries of race science by offering a burgeoning plethora of such "characteristics." *The Secret Doctrine*'s use of ethnological categories vacates them of classificatory content and specificity, instead injecting them with a fantastical, algebraic logic, according to which various races either derive from or tend toward (or both derive from and tend toward) one another. In so doing, Theosophy holds up a mortifying mirror to the rhetoric and logic of race science, calling ethnological arguments into question precisely because its mimicry of their logic is organized around unverifiable claims to authority and initiation that reflect back on ethnology's own structures of evidence.

We can also see how these abstract reimaginings of race reflect back on the very identity categories that so fascinated philologists at this time and, in so

---

[73] That said, the Theosophical deployment of "Aryan" has been described as an influence on history's most dangerously literal reading of the Aryan hypothesis. Nicholas Goodrick-Clark argues that Nazism derived some of its most pernicious ideas from the German movement of "Ariosophy," which was in turn influenced by Theosophy and *The Secret Doctrine*. As Goodrick-Clark writes, Ariosophists like Guido von List (1848–1919) and Jörg Lanz von Liebenfels (1874–1954) "combined German *völkisch* nationalism and racism with occult notions borrowed from the theosophy of Helena Petrovna Blavatsky, in order to prophesy and vindicate a coming era of German world rule" (Goodrick-Clark, *Occult Roots*, p. 2).

[74] Risseuw, "Thinking Culture," p. 199.

doing, create new ways of framing the nineteenth-century workings of race (and consequently, as we will see, of caste). In an essay on the influence of spiritualist and occultist ideas on anthropology, Peter Pels writes that "at about the same time that the Theosophical Society was founded (1875), the originally 'oriental' Aryan was transformed into the blond and blue-eyed image of what was to become one of the most frightening forms of modern racism."[75] At the critical pivot-point of the late nineteenth century, chronologically about halfway between the zenith of Romantic Indomania and the twentieth century's malignant Nazi reformulation of the Aryan hypothesis, the Theosophical Society offered its own esoteric reformulations of the philological concept.

In *The Secret Doctrine*, we see Blavatsky diverge from the philological approach somewhat. The term "Aryan" accommodates the cosmological in the racial, as Blavatsky cites the authority of her Masters to repurpose it into a technical term within her esoteric macrohistory.[76] Theosophical geography also departs from both the Orientalist model and the subsequent theories of race science, by situating the original Aryan homeland in India and identifying Indians as Aryans, in line with the beliefs of late-nineteenth-century Hindu revivalists like Swami Dayananda Saraswati and Swami Vivekananda.[77] Even so, Blavatsky's *Isis Unveiled* often seems to refer the category of Aryan back to philology's classifications by opposing it to the Semitic stream, which further enables an attack upon Christianity.

> Out of all the sacred writings of all the branch nations, sprung from the primitive stock of mankind, Christianity must choose for its guidance the national records and scriptures of a people perhaps the least spiritual of the human family – the Semitic. A branch that has never been able to develop out of its numerous tongues a language capable of embodying ideas of a moral and intellectual world; whose form of expression and drift of thought could never soar higher than the purely sensual and terrestrial figures of speech; whose literature has left nothing original, nothing that was not borrowed from the Aryan thought; and whose science and philosophy are utterly wanting in those noble features which characterize the highly spiritual and metaphysical systems of the Indo-European (Japetic) races.[78]

---

[75] Pels, "Occult Truths," p. 12.

[76] Others who have applied the term "macrohistory" to Theosophy's master narratives of the past include Trompf, "Theosophical Macrohistory," and Viswanathan, "In Search of Madame Blavatsky."

[77] Bryant quotes an 1881 talk that Olcott delivered to Indian audiences, in which he argues for a renewal of Romantic Orientalist ideas: "The theory that Aryavarta was the cradle of European civilization, the Aryans the progenitors of western peoples … is comparatively a thing of yesterday. Professor Max Müller and … other Sanskritists … have been bringing about this change in western ideas. Let us hope that before many years roll by, we may have out the whole truth about Aryan civilization, and that your ancestors (and ours) will be honoured according to their deserts" (Bryant, *Quest*, pp. 21–22).

[78] Blavatsky, *Isis Unveiled Vol. 2*, p. 435.

In other words, the Semitic is exoteric and sensual, the Aryan esoteric and metaphysical.[79] As with some of the most influential scholarly variations on the Aryan-Semitic theme, Blavatsky's attack on Christianity jumbles religion, race, and language: not only does she apply the philological classifications of "Indo-European," "Japetic," "Aryan," and "Semitic" as racial categories, but the logic of such distinctions is to be found in a racialized use of language, and, in turn, the types of religious experience the different linguistic traits enable. Blavatsky's distinctions hark back to Ernest Renan's taxonomy of religions, according to which the Semites are intrinsically monotheistic, while the Aryans are polytheistic, mythological, and more inclined to abstract philosophizing – precisely the attitude that Müller had rejected in "Semitic Monotheism."[80]

Moreover, what seems to be simply an abstract, computational vision of esoteric world-systems in *The Secret Doctrine* – one whose use of the term "race" seems near-synonymous with broader term like "beings" or "species" and, as we have noted, reads as a wild allegory of race science itself – in the process also enacts a logic that could best be characterized as eugenic. In one such instance, Blavatsky describes "Malays, Papuans and Hottentots" as racial errors, identifying them as the unfortunate result of crossings between the seventh subrace of the third (Lemurian) root race and the earliest subraces of the fourth (Atlantean) root race.[81] In the various descriptions of those subraces that currently inhabit Earth (or "Globe D" as it is known in the text), Blavatsky borrows freely from contemporary ethnological and anthropological discourse, even as she disputes their findings; for instance, when she writes that "the occult doctrine admits of no such divisions as the Aryan and the Semite .... The Semites ... are later Aryans – degenerate in spirituality and perfected in materiality. To these belong all the Jews and the Arabs. The former are a tribe descended from the Chandalas of India, the outcasts."[82] Blavatsky strongly and

---

[79] In fact, many of Blavatsky's writings – from the 1875 articles in the spiritualist press to the posthumous fifth volume of *The Secret Doctrine* – discuss the esotericism of the Jewish Kabala, and even describe the Talmud and Kabala as the key to Christianity's real meaning. Blavatsky frequently draws comparisons between Judaism and "Oriental" religions, only to find the former lacking because of its gross sexuality and "phallic nature." In *Esoteric Writings*, she repeats the idea that Jewish hermeneutics are sophisticated, but in service of an overtly sexualized esoteric symbology; thus, the Aryans "used their Science of Correspondences to veil the most spiritual and sublime truths of Nature," but Jews only talk of "birth" and "generation" (Blavatsky, *Esoteric Writings*, p. 77).

[80] While I discuss Max Müller more in this Element, Renan is an important figure in the establishment of comparative religion in the nineteenth century. Olender quotes Renan thus: "Originally Jewish to the core, Christianity over time rid itself of nearly everything it took from the race, so that those who consider Christianity to be the Aryan religion par excellence are in many respects correct" (quoted in Olender, *Languages*, p. 70).

[81] Blavatsky, *Secret Doctrine Vol. 2*, p. 697. For more on the Theosophical incorporation of "lost" places like Lemuria and Atlantis, see Chapter 3, "Occult Losses," in Ramaswamy, *The Lost Land of Lemuria*.

[82] Blavatsky, *Secret Doctrine Vol. 2*, p. 178.

explicitly disputes the Orientalist conception of Aryans and Semites from her occultist vantage point – but almost simultaneously constructs a narrative of degeneration that both relates and distinguishes Semites and Aryans, implicitly accepting the "division" crafted by Orientalist philology. We see here, too, a glimpse of the fusion of race science and caste, as "materialist" Jews are called the descendants of so-called untouchables or "outcasts." Anti-Semitism and casteism meet among the root races.[83]

## 3.3 Occulting Caste

Clearly, even as the specific generic and formal instability of Blavatsky's texts allows us to read against the grain of their Aryanist assertions, and even though she stoutly objects to certain Orientalist classifications, *The Secret Doctrine* participates in the contemporary discourse of race and caste. While Blavatsky's incorporations of contemporary racial categories have received their share of critical attention, it is worth considering the related – and relatively neglected – question of how caste shows up in her writings: all the more so, for our purposes, given that it reflects back the simultaneous influence of both Orientalist ethnology and of Theosophy's Indian interlocutors. Of course, race and caste are not disconnected, or solely parallel entities – in fact, if the hypothesis of the Aryan family had ramifications for the European view of race, it also reshaped the understanding of the caste system in India, including for Indians themselves.[84]

In the reconfigured genealogies of "Anthropogenesis," and in Blavatsky's writings more broadly, we glimpse a clear interrelation between the text's assumed Aryanism and the broader matter of caste. In fantastically conflating the lineage of the "degenerate" Jew with that of the subjugated Indian Chandalas, for example, Theosophy imaginatively paraphrases, as kinship relation, decades of Indological (and more broadly, Orientalist) speculation on the relationship between race and caste as refracted through the Aryan family theory. Gail Omvedt has written that "the 'Aryan theory of race' originated by European Orientalists" became "an ideological legitimation of the system of caste hierarchy."[85] This "ideological legitimation" occurred through Orientalism's stories of the past as well as in its redefinitions of the textual archive – particularly in relation to the preeminence it granted certain texts such as the *Bhagavad Gita*.

---

[83] For an overview of the politics involved in the terminology of "Untouchable," "Dalit," and "Bahujan," please see Guru, "The Politics of Naming."

[84] Romila Thapar suggests that this reconfigured identity emerges out of the collaboration between Orientalists and their Brahmanical sources: "The Aryan identity was encouraged by the pre-eminence given to the Vedas by the Brahmanical tradition which also ensured that they became the primary texts for European scholars working on Indian civilization" (Thapar, "Multiple Theories," p. 35).

[85] Omvedt, *Dalits*, p. 15.

It is worth noting that the crucial significance of caste's relationship to race extends far beyond the nineteenth century, and continues to be a vexed matter of debate (as well as a productive locus of transcultural political solidarities), well into our own time. It came into focus, for example, in 2001, when Dalit activists fought to classify casteist discrimination as a site of racism at the UN World Conference against Racism, Racial Discrimination, Xenophobia, and Related Intolerance at Durban, South Africa. More recently, in *Caste: The Origins of our Discrimination*, Isabel Wilkerson argues that anti-black racism in the United States is best understood as the manifestation of an American caste system, since caste is an assumed and "invisible grammar" of the sort that underlies "the language of race."[86] In considering ideological paradigms that legitimate this "invisible grammar," Wilkerson turns to the examples par excellence of Nazi Aryan theory (with its own genocidal phantasmagoria of Semitic degeneracy) and the Laws of Manu, which codified and ranked the four *varnas* or strata of the Hindu caste system.

The fingerprints of Orientalism are evident here, too. The *Manusmriti* (the Laws of Manu) was one of the first Sanskrit texts William Jones translated in 1776, as British officials of the East India Company under the guidance of Warren Hastings, the first Governor-General of Bengal, sought a primary textual resource for Hindu personal law. As Rita Kothari and Krupa Shah point out, the "translation of ancient texts believed to be the unchanging repositories of 'Hindu law' became indispensable" for the purposes of colonial administration.[87] We also see here the crux of the Saidian critique of Orientalism, since the task of translation was inextricable, for Jones, from his professional roles as a judge and administrator, and had far-reaching material consequences for millions of Indians. The first English translation of the *Manusmriti* transformed it from one among many ancient legal texts into a singular cornerstone of Hindu law, which could then act as the legitimizing primary source, in legal terms, for all aspects of Hindu social existence – most significantly, of caste, since the *Manusmriti* lays down the laws of the four main classes of the Hindu caste system. Susan Bayly suggests that Jones erroneously believed the *Manusmriti* to be a quintessentially Aryan text dating back to early Vedic times, and viewed the "primordial Aryans as heroes of a great adventure of migration and conquest 'at the earliest dawn

---

[86] Wilkerson, *Caste*, p. 18. Wilkerson writes, too, of the rich history of solidarity between the Dalit and the African American communities: In the nineteenth century, the anti-caste activist Jyotiba Phule drew inspiration from the success of African American abolitionists; in the mid-twentieth century, the architect of the Indian constitution, B. R. Ambedkar (another founding figure of the anti-caste movement) famously corresponded with the author and civil rights leader W. E. B. Du Bois about the solidarity of Dalits and African Americans (Wilkerson, *Caste*, p. 26).

[87] Kothari and Shah, "More or Less," p. 135.

of history,' bringing with them from their west Asian homeland the teachings of a divine law-giver, Manu."[88] In other words, the Aryans are imagined as both authoring and authorizing the foundational logic of the caste system – or to return to Omvedt's description, precisely providing "ideological legitimation" for the caste system, under the aegis of Indological scholarship and translation.

Over the course of the nineteenth century and with the further racialization of the Aryan theory, it is possible to trace "an emerging ethnological orthodoxy" in which Brahmins and other upper-caste Hindus were descended from the Aryan invaders of India, while the indigenous "Dravidians" of India had remained outcastes.[89] The implication, clearly compatible with a colonial outlook, is that, despite being of the same "superior" stock as the British, these Aryans over time degenerated into ignorance and superstition and, unlike their white relatives, adopted the oppressive structure of the caste system. And yet, at the same time, despite this seeming denunciation of caste, the logic of the conception is itself casteist, given that it identifies Brahmins as Aryan and thus superior to the other castes. In other words, even as the actions of earlier Orientalists like Jones effectively consolidated the Laws of Manu and its caste diktats as the keystone of Hindu law – and even as nineteenth-century ethnology regularly presented Brahmins and other upper castes as distant kin to the British, therefore assuming caste to be the very ground of their Aryan kinship with Indians[90] – evangelicals, colonial scholar-officials, and intellectuals like James Mill also criticized the caste system as evidence of Hinduism's "degrading superstitions" and degeneration, and therefore justification for British rule.[91] Colonial discourse has its casteist cake and reprovingly eats it, too.

As happens so often, Theosophy also holds a mirror to both of these attitudes to caste, simultaneously – although the optic it offers is often more funhouse mirror than looking glass. The taxonomical impulse dominating Victorian ethnology, which also influenced the colonial study of Indian castes, religious communities, and tribes, finds itself reflected in the sprawling, eccentric classifications and genealogies that constitute Blavatsky's cosmologies. Theosophy's self-presentation as an esoteric movement complicates and compounds its Orientalist derivations. In writing about the evolution of root races, Blavatsky seems to sublimate the rationale of caste into her otherworldly metahistory, by building an elaborate, hierarchical system that operates through heredity and evolution. Caste becomes an occulted model for Theosophy's racial taxonomies

[88] Bayly, *Caste, Society, and Politics*, p. 114.   [89] Bayly, "Caste and 'Race'," p.170.

[90] As Peter van der Veer writes, "the notion that the higher castes of India belonged to the same Aryan race as the British was widely accepted" by this time (van der Veer, *Imperial Encounters*, p. 49).

[91] Bayly, "Caste and 'Race'," p. 127.

as well as in its historical master narratives.[92] Nor is this a matter of rough analogy – in fact, Blavatsky repurposes the caste system in her very conception of esotericism. Theosophy's theory of the secret doctrine *turns on* the notion that only the initiated and the truly elect may have access to an arcane and ancient wisdom – both in the self-evident sense of the phrase (that this is the axis upon which Theosophy revolves), and in the less obvious and contradictory sense that Theosophy, at another level, also turns against this much-touted axiom, since its very mission is to make public and widely accessible the ancient, secret doctrine. Even so, Blavatsky's writings never let go of the boast and glamor of initiated esotericism: as such, the caste system stands as a readymade model of hierarchical exclusivity, too easily available for her not to adapt and appropriate for her purposes at several points. In *Isis Unveiled*, for instance, she writes that "the true interpretation" of metempsychosis, "discussed at length in Manu and the Buddhistic sacred books," is bound to have been widely misunderstood, "having been confined from the first to the learned sacerdotal castes."[93] The definitive exclusivity that attends a "true" understanding of religious texts here is effortlessly coextensive with the caste system.

Moreover, Blavatsky's placement of Manu and "the Buddhistic sacred books" on the same plane comes across as a significant mischaracterization, given that the Buddha broke from the Brahminical social system to found a more egalitarian order. While a shift of this sort is in keeping with Blavatsky's inventive approach to historical genealogies (and nominal identities) more generally – and as such, challenges the official historiography by diverging from it – this representation also has more far-reaching implications for the larger question of caste and race hierarchy. The anti-casteist bite of Buddhism finds itself defanged here, as Blavatsky reinscribes the Buddha into the Hindu caste system that he rejected, and instead describes him as an upper-caste "Aryan" who learnt from "initiated Brahmins."

> [T]he reader is asked to bear in mind the very important difference between orthodox Buddhism – i.e., the public teachings of Gautama the Buddha, and his esoteric Budhism. His Secret Doctrine, however, differed in no wise from that of the initiated Brahmins of his day. The Buddha was a child of the Aryan soil; a born Hindu, a Kshatrya and a disciple of the "twice born" (the initiated Brahmins) or Dwijas.[94] His teachings, therefore, could not be different from

---

[92] Caste is not the only source of hierarchy at work: Like many other late-Victorian occultist organizations, the Society is also influenced by Freemasonry and other esoteric formations. My suggestion is simply that the racialized content of Theosophy's hierarchies implicitly folds in the logic of caste – a relation hitherto neglected.

[93] Blavatsky, *Isis Unveiled Vol. 2*, p. 279.

[94] It may be useful to unpack Blavatsky's citation of "twice-born" as synonymous with Brahmins. In her expansive "alternative history" of Hindu society (one that seeks to include non-Brahmanical

> their doctrines, for the whole Buddhist reform merely consisted in giving out a portion of that which had been kept secret from every man outside of the "enchanted" circle of Temple-Initiates and ascetics. Unable to teach all that had been imparted to him – owing to his pledges – though he taught a philosophy built upon the ground-work of the true esoteric knowledge, the Buddha gave to the world only its outward material body and kept its soul for his Elect.[95]

By clipping off a "d" from "Buddhism" and abstracting it to "Budhism" (allying it to the Sanskrit "buddhi," meaning "wisdom," rather than the historical personage, Gautama Buddha), Blavatsky suggests that the esoteric doctrine smuggled into Buddhism is no "different from [Brahminical] doctrines": she recapitulates caste orthodoxy by suggesting that the Buddha's seemingly egalitarian creed belongs to the realm of the "body," whereas the initiatic, ascetic, quasi-Brahmin "soul" of his beliefs is kept for the "Elect." Here, Theosophical esotericism adjusts itself to flow along the prefabricated channels offered by the caste system.

And yet, even as she revels in the mystique of "the learned and sacerdotal castes," extols the legacy of Manu, or, as here, demotes Buddhist reformism to the level of "outward material body" – in other words, even as she implicitly extends the logic of caste – Blavatsky also elsewhere explicitly rejects the caste system as corrupt, dogmatic, and degenerate, just as many British and European observers and writers did in their denunciation of "Brahmanism." In a piece called "Misconceptions" published in the French monthly *Le Lotus* in 1887, Blavatsky responded to a critique of the Theosophical Society (and its Indian, Hindu allegiances) by a votary of western occultism writing under the pen name "Aleph."[96] "Misconceptions" repeats the idea of "esoteric Budhism," but over the course of her defense of Theosophy, Blavatsky launches a frontal assault on the caste system. Putting some distance between her organization and the Hindu practices that Aleph's original critique apparently attacked, she dismisses the devotees of the Hindu deity Jagannath as suicidally "ignorant," and blames their upper-caste oppressors for perverting the truth of "the esoteric philosophy."

---

and Orientalist-inflected aspects of ancient Hindu culture), Wendy Doniger writes that in the Vedic era, "[t]he three upper classes were called twice born because of the second birth through the ritual of initiation (the ancient Indian equivalent of becoming born again), in which a man was born (again) as a fully developed member of the community" – and yet, that while "Brahmins may have had a monopoly on liturgical Sanskrit for the performance of certain public rites," they were not the only ones granted the status of "twice-born" (Doniger, *Hindus*, p. 37).

[95] Blavatsky, *Secret Doctrine Vol. 1*, p. 4.

[96] According to the editors of the volume that reprinted this piece, "Aleph" was the nom de plume of Charles Limousin, who seems to have been a journalist, Fourierist, and Freemason. The nature of Blavatsky's responses suggests that Aleph's attack was on the "intellectual derangement and ... jugglery" represented by the Indian affinities of the Theosophical Society (Blavatsky, "Misconceptions," p. 2).

> Asceticism, as understood by exoteric religions, has produced the ignorant
> fools who throw themselves under the chariot of Juggernaut. If these unfor-
> tunate people had studied the esoteric philosophy, they would know that
> under the dead letter of the dogma taught by the Brâhmanas – exploiters,
> like all priests, inheritors of the possessions of their victims, who are driven to
> madness by superstitious terrors – is hidden a profoundly philosophical
> meaning.[97]

Here, Blavatsky's rejection of a corrupt priesthood is reminiscent of the broader Victorian denunciation of the Hindu caste system as superstitious, quasi-"Papish," and in need of reform; to this, she adds the additional allegation that the priestly caste is stuck in the mire of exotericism, unable to reach the true, concealed meaning of Hindu philosophy that her Masters have shared with her, which is the same as the "*Universal Esotericism* preserved by certain cosmopolitan fraternities"[98] or the "'Ancient Wisdom' of the Ante-Vedic Âryas."[99] Whereas the trope of an exclusive and initiated fraternity often slides into the idea of upper-caste savants in *The Secret Doctrine* and other writings, in "Misconceptions," the Brahmins are emphatically not part of an inner circle. Moreover, the true kernel of "esoteric philosophy" is not simply or solely Hindu (or Brahminical), but rather a transcultural doctrine shared by "certain cosmopolitan fraternities," reaching for universality. Blavatsky goes on to present Theosophy as the means to a broader reform and revival of Hindu ancient wisdom, both through its esoteric understanding of the perennial wisdom, and its embodiment of a belief in "Universal Brotherhood" (which rids it of the trappings of caste inequality). Much of the essay presents current-day Brahmins as opportunistic and corrupt, and Blavatsky acknowledges Aleph to be "dead right" about "Brâhmanism," before offering the promise of a future Aryan family reunion hosted by Theosophy.

> Yes, exoteric Brâhmanism must fall, but it will be replaced by esoteric
> Vedism, to which will be added everything noble and beautiful that progres-
> sive science has evolved in this last century. But this revolution will not be
> accomplished by conquerors; it is by means of brotherly love that the fusion
> of the two Âryan races will be brought about, and only when the Englishman
> will have ceased to look upon the Brâhmana – whose genealogical tree
> encompasses three thousand years – as the representative of an inferior
> race . . .. The brotherhood of the Theosophists throughout India are the only
> ones to see the haughty Englishman sitting down at the same table with
> equally arrogant Brâhmanas, mellowed and humanized by the example and
> the lessons of the Theosophists who serve the Masters of the Ancient

---

[97] Blavatsky, "Misconceptions," p. 5.    [98] Blavatsky, "Misconceptions," p. 6.
[99] Blavatsky, "Misconceptions," p. 8.

> Wisdom, the descendants of those Rishis and Mahâtmas which Brâhmanism
> has always revered, though it has ceased to understand them.[100]

Here is the longed-for coming together of estranged Aryan brothers, finally seated together at the Theosophical table and equal in their postures of entitlement. If the end of *The Coming Race* anticipated apocalypse at the hands of an advanced branch of the Aryan family, Blavatsky's vision of the future departs from that fictional inspiration by imagining a happy "fusion of the two Âryan races" under Theosophy's auspices. Moreover, in keeping with the rest of "Misconceptions," which explicitly opposes the caste system, Blavatsky predicts the end of "exoteric Brâhmanism" as the excrescences of superstition fall away, leaving behind a perfect blend of the esoteric truth of the "Ancient Wisdom" and modern occultism or "progressive science." And yet, in the very same paragraph, as we have seen, Blavatsky assumes a 3,000-year-old "genealogical tree" to be reason enough to exonerate "Brâhmanism" from the charge of inferiority. It is a move that smuggles the hereditary logic of caste back into her attack on European racial arrogance – and on the caste system itself. Nor does the text seem to register that to reject "exoteric Brâhmanism" in favor of "esoteric Vedism" reinscribes the hierarchies of the caste system, given that the Vedas – the oldest scriptural texts written in Sanskrit – are themselves synonymous with Brahminical culture; traditionally, only upper castes were able to access the Sanskrit language of the Vedas, and Brahmins were considered the "custodians of the Veda."[101] In insisting upon a distinction between pure "esoteric Vedism" and corrupt "exoteric Brâhmanism," Blavatsky is not challenging caste hierarchy so much as romanticizing its origins through her celebration of an Aryan ancient wisdom that dates back to the Vedic age, despite her clear denunciation of modern-day Brahmanism.

In this celebration, Blavatsky echoes the views of the Hindu revivalist Arya Samaj, a reformist society with which the Theosophical Society briefly collaborated. Rejecting the rituals and polytheistic profusion of orthodox Hinduism, the founder of the Arya Samaj, Swami Dayananda Saraswati, promoted a more austere, monistic practice based on the values of Vedic philosophy. Theosophy's encounter with the Swami was significant; in fact, when Olcott and Blavatsky

---

[100] Blavatsky, "Misconceptions," pp. 23–24.

[101] This description is worth quoting in full. Wendy Doniger writes that one early definition of the "Hindus" as a group might have been those who "called themselves the people of the Veda, or the people who revere the Brahmins who are the custodians of the Veda. ... Or they called themselves the Aryas ('nobles') in contrast with the Dasyus or Dasas ('aliens' or 'slaves') or barbarians (*mlechhas*)" (Doniger, *Hindus*, p. 26). She also explains that the overwhelmingly textual bias in the European approach to Hinduism led to a casteist bias: "the Orientalist orientation to texts is the orientation towards Brahmins (and Sanskrit, and writing)" (Doniger, *Hindus*, p. 34).

first went to India in 1878, they temporarily rechristened their organization "the Theosophical Society of the Arya Samaj," although the two groups soon proved to be incompatible partners, falling out in public by 1882. The Swami was unable to stomach either Olcott and Blavatsky's interest in occultism or their embrace of Buddhism, while the Theosophists were dismayed by the Arya Samaj's commitment to a narrowly Hindu creed.[102] Nevertheless, both societies continued to share the belief that India, or "Aryavarta," was the original homeland of the Aryans; as such, both disagreed with the academic Orientalist belief in an Aryan invasion of India. In envisioning India as the origin and home of all other religions, Romila Thapar suggests, Theosophy was influenced by Swami Dayananda's conviction that Vedanta was, in fact, "the source of all knowledge."[103]

Even after the two societies parted ways, we see the continuing influence of the Arya Samaj on Theosophical conceptions of caste.[104] In the introductory sections of *The Secret Doctrine*, for instance, Blavatsky writes about the ancient wisdom that was transmitted down the ages and across civilizations: "the universally diffused religion of the ancient and prehistoric world," preserved in the "crypts" of mysterious libraries.[105] Tellingly, she cites Dayananda as she envisions a future in which these archives, saved and secreted by "the Occult Fraternity," may be widely shared – "safe from Western spoliating hands, to reappear in some more enlightened age, for which in the words of the late Swami Dayanand Sarasvati, 'the *Mlechhas* (outcasts, savages, those beyond the pale of Aryan civilization) will have to wait.'"[106] The untranslated term, "*mlechha*," Sanskrit for alien or invader and roughly equivalent to "barbarian," becomes a marker of otherness that (as Blavatsky's gloss of the term as "outcasts" suggests) preserves the exclusionary structure of caste.

Both *The Secret Doctrine* and "Misconceptions" came out some years after Dayananda's death, but as we have seen, Blavatsky continued to cite him. Ultimately, the Arya Samaj modeled a form of ambivalence around caste for the Theosophical Society, campaigning against untouchability while holding on

---

[102] See the account of this schism in Sand, "The Marriage between the Theosophical Society and the Arya Samaj."

[103] Thapar discusses this in her "Foreword" to *Aryans and British India* (Trautmann, *Aryans*, p. xiv). Elsewhere, Thapar has argued that the Theosophical Society's identification of India as the homeland of the Aryans and identification of the Aryans as "the progenitors of Indian civilization" was taken up by Hindu revivalists and continues to form a spectral presence in current Hindu supremacist rhetoric (Thapar, "Theory of Aryan Race," p. 1115).

[104] We also see the influence of Orientalist philology and ethnology on beliefs of the Arya Samaj – at the most obvious level, in the very use of the term "Arya" in the organization's name, and its mobilization of the Orientalist category of the Aryan, and in the Arya Samaj's idealization of a glorious Aryan civilization.

[105] Blavatsky, *Secret Doctrine Vol. 1*, p. 14.    [106] Blavatsky, *Secret Doctrine Vol. 1*, p. 14.

to the basic hierarchy of caste.[107] We find Blavatsky echoing the Swami's belief in a Hindu reform based on a return to the Vedas. In espousing a caste system supposedly based on merit rather than heredity (in other words, by ignoring the working of historical privilege), and in its enthusiasm for the Vedic past, the Arya Samaj stopped short of a real critique of caste ideology.[108] We see this reflected in Blavatsky's approach, though "Misconceptions" speaks out against social injustice not only in India but also in the West.

All told, caste must be understood as a significant, albeit understudied, influence on Theosophy's esoteric hierarchies and classifications. Even so, Theosophy ultimately continues to speak for the broadly utopian horizon of "Universal Brotherhood" in ways that push through these typologies. Even within *The Secret Doctrine*, which revels in hierarchy and exclusivity, we can see casteist formulations being fabricated along fantastical genealogies, part of an epic cosmology that often reads, with its discussion of root races or virtual globes, like broad speculative fiction. *Isis Unveiled*, as we have noted, with its nominality of classification, indifference to consistency around identity, and accommodation of esoteric histories, also effectively undermines the purism of the Arya Samaj worldview. Theosophy's expansive syncretism and interest in occult science are precisely the traits that warned Dayananda Saraswati off a fusion between the two societies.

For Theosophy's purposes, Dayananda might be thought of as a "native informant," to cite Viswanathan's description of the Masters, who allowed Blavatsky to challenge the scholarly authority of expert Indologists.[109] Blavatsky's contestation of academic Orientalism, of course, hinges on the idea that the archives and libraries on which philologists and scholars of comparative religion depend are unable to match the knowledge of initiated practitioners. Dayananda becomes an authority that she mobilizes to challenge the chronology of the Orientalists or the worth of their textual archive. In the same introduction to *The Secret Doctrine*, for example, Blavatsky suggests that

---

[107] As Susan Bayly writes, Swami Dayananda Saraswati "conceived of the regenerated 'Aryan' nation as a domain of purified Hindu piety in which classifications of varnā, which were portrayed as hierarchical grades of moral affiliation, would be assigned to each sharer in the vedic faith of 'Aryavarta' on the basis of the individual's learning and other personal attainments" (Bayly, "Hindu Modernisers," p. 107).

[108] It is worth recalling that caste is itself not a singular framework, and it refers to at least two conceptions of the social order. The ideology of *varna*, or the four strata that we find in the *Manusmriti*, intersects with a more numerous, less fixed form of social grouping called *jati*. Even if the Arya Samaj expressed a critique of caste injustice, Roland Lardinois points out that its "writings value the *varna* system to the detriment of the *jati*, according to the old idea that caste (assimilated to varna) is a matter of merit and not of birth" (Lardinois, "The Idea of Caste," p. 40).

[109] Viswanathan, "Ordinary Business," p. 13. Viswanathan borrows the term from anthropology, applying it to Blavatsky's "Masters" to say that they played the part of "facilitating" and guiding her, unlike Orientalist scholars who relied solely on a textual archive.

"Eastern initiates" could access texts that were completely unknown to the philologists. In this, she cites both "a prominent Cinghalese priest" and "the late Swami Dayanand Sarasvati, the greatest Sanskritist of his day in India," describing the laughter of the "holy and learned man" when told that Müller had said he had found no textual evidence of ancient revelation.

> His answer was suggestive. "If Mr. *Moksh Mooller*, as he pronounced the name, were a Brahmin, and came with me, I might take him to a gupta cave (a secret crypt) near Okhee Math, in the Himalayas, where he would soon find out that what crossed the Kalapani (the black waters of the ocean) from India to Europe were only the bits of rejected copies of some passages from our sacred books."[110]

Evidently, the Swami's dismissal of "Mr Moksh Mooller" is inextricable from the fact that the Professor is not a Brahmin, and must therefore be denied a visit to the secret Himalayan crypt. The author of *The Secret Doctrine,* as she offers Dayananda's posthumous words, seems to revel in the simultaneous put-down of the eminent Indologist and in the esotericism of "Brahmanism." (Curiously, it seems not to cross her mind that she herself is no Brahmin – perhaps because, as an initiate of the Masters, she floats along on the astral plane far above these mundane matters, requiring nothing more than her own psychic powers to access the great archives of the occult.) Despite the shifts and variations in Blavatsky's views, it is possible to see a steady consistency, at least, in her stated critiques of scholars of comparative religion and language, even as she cites and draws from their work. By quoting Dayananda's scathing dismissal of Müller in the introductory section of her monumental work, Blavatsky signals that *The Secret Doctrine* is a challenge to the findings of philology.

Theosophy's ambiguity around caste stands for us as an illustrative example of Blavatsky's typical dodge-and-weave: frequently, we see her assert a certain claim that then invites some form of criticism from either Orientalists or occultists (e.g., that she does not have the requisite archival expertise, or that there is a regressive tendency in Theosophy's eastward drift). Often, in defense, Blavatsky will go on to contradict an earlier position in order to evade the accusation. If this is her usual "dodge," the Blavatsky "weave" refers, punningly, to her simultaneous swerve away from previous statements and her working together of myriad eclectic sources into the fabric of Theosophical theory. In that many-stranded tapestry, one finds anti-colonial reform discourse laced together with colonial scholarship; one finds imaginings of caste and race that claim an almost cosmic logic; and yet, one also finds their categories unraveled, transformed, and knotted anew.

---

[110] Blavatsky, *Secret Doctrine Vol. 1*, p. 11.

## 4 Dissonance and Resonance

In focusing on caste and its constructions within Blavatsky's writings, we have been able to trace Theosophy's fraught and complex representations of a deeply consequential category of social and political identity. That complexity both magnifies – on to the plane of the visionary – and reflects the contradictions and elisions around caste in academic Orientalist accounts themselves, particularly those that are refracted through the Aryan family hypothesis and race theory. We see that there is no simple verdict to be passed, no way of foreclosing the heterogeneity and incoherence of the whole discursive field. In closely reading the relationship between Theosophy and Orientalism through the case of caste, we see, also, that the basic narrative of history is up for grabs.

It comes as no surprise, then, that Blavatsky's writings feature such abrasive outbursts against Indologists as we see against Müller in *The Secret Doctrine*. It would be easy to dismiss this critique as a one-sided, marginal fixation, given the relative cultural authoritativeness of comparative philology and comparative religion. And yet, Orientalists in turn commented on Theosophical ideas about religions like Buddhism and Vedanta. Müller, for instance, seems to have found it impossible to ignore Blavatsky's view of Theosophy as an alternative form of comparative, transcultural study.[111] In this section of the Element, we will examine ways in which Müller's work engages with the esoteric Orientalism of Theosophy, before also considering the mystical-syncretic strains within his own work.

## 4.1 Arguing in Print

During the summer of 1893 (after Blavatsky's death), Müller published two articles on Theosophy in *The Nineteenth Century*.[112] Within the opening pages of the first piece, the author sets up the esoteric and philological approaches to

---

[111] Müller, in fact, also gave several lectures in 1892, later collected as *Theosophy Or Psychological Religion*, which argued against the esotericist approach to comparative religion. He also championed a more traditional understanding of "theosophy," positing it, as Thomas Green writes, against "the 'humbuggery'" of Theosophy and similar movements: "Müller described true religion as 'theosophy' – the union of humanity and divinity – and argued that the Hindus possessed theosophy in its purest form in the Vedānta, an ancient exegetical tradition focused on the Upanishads" (Green, "Spirit," p. 230).

[112] For more on this exchange, see Donald S. Lopez, Jr., "Orientalist vs. Theosophist," an essay in *Imagining the East* that draws our attention to the contending views of Müller and Olcott, specifically, in the western imagination of Buddhism. Apart from discussing Sinnett's 1883 book, *Esoteric Buddhism*, Lopez also delves into the same exchange in *The Nineteenth Century* that I discuss here, suggesting that the central question of who can speak for the Buddha is the galvanizing force behind "the obscure exchange between two late Victorians, one an aged Oxford Sanskritist and the other, at least in view of some, an embittered spiritualist quack" (Lopez, "Orientalist vs. Theosophist," p. 47). Lopez further identifies Sinnett's larger approach to the Buddha's caste-blindness as "an act of cosmic colonialism," since Sinnett's esoteric

Indic religions as a contest. Müller begins by mockingly paraphrasing the esotericist claim "that there are native scholars in possession of mysteries of which we poor professors have no conception," pointing out that these mysteries seem available only to those without knowledge of Sanskrit and Pali: an ignorance that – as he sarcastically notes – "seems to be the first condition for being admitted to the esoteric wisdom of India."[113] One might sense a personal edge to this biting retort, and it is entirely possible that he was smarting over the stinging rebukes that Blavatsky formulated, and relayed from Dayananda Saraswati to "Mr. Moksh Mooller." As we will see, Müller cites precisely those opening portions of *The Secret Doctrine*, which also expound the notion of "esoteric Budhism" (with one "d," as in "Misconceptions"). At any rate, neither of his two critics is spared. Müller writes that when Blavatsky first went to India, "she thought that she had found at last what she wanted in Dayânanda Sarasvati ... no doubt a remarkable and powerful mind" – but, as Müller also writes (lest the affirmation of this praise be taken as unequivocal), "it can no longer be doubted that Dayânanda Sarasvati was as deficient in moral straightforwardness" as Blavatsky herself.[114] As we see in these brief excerpts, therefore, Müller seems to have been as dismissive of Blavatsky and the Swami, if more politely so, as they were of him.

After explicating the ways in which the doctrines and writings of Theosophy are misguided and rife with error, Müller comes to a significant grouse: that Blavatsky's following "has become so large ... that the movement started by her can no longer be ignored."[115] Müller's objection to the popularity and influence of Theosophy centers on what he sees as the subsequent spread of misinformation, such as the idea of "esoteric Buddhism." It is a term that Müller rejects as oxymoronic, given Buddhism's fundamental commitment to making its precepts and practices freely available, regardless of caste; as he puts it, "if there is any religion entirely free from esoteric doctrines it is Buddhism. There never was any such thing as mystery in Buddhism."[116] The article does accept the Theosophical criticism that his own scholarship relies excessively on texts rather than experience or "native" instruction – as Müller acknowledges, he has never actually been to India – but he counters that those with little knowledge of the languages of Indian religious texts are ill equipped to make claims about Vedanta and Buddhism.

---

chronology has the Buddha reborn as a Śamkara, who was in fact a "great persecutor of Buddhism" (Lopez, "Orientalist vs. Theosophist," p. 51).

[113] Müller, "Esoteric Buddhism," p. 767.    [114] Müller, "Esoteric Buddhism," p. 770.

[115] See Müller, "Esoteric Buddhism," p. 772. Thereafter, A. P. Sinnett wrote "Reply," followed by "Rejoinder," in which Müller seems to have had the last word.

[116] Müller, "Esoteric Buddhism," p. 776.

Müller's piece in *The Nineteenth Century* thus doubles and flips Blavatsky's own critiques, by framing Orientalism's disagreement with Theosophy as a contest between linguistic and textual knowledge on the one hand, and unsubstantiated claims to initiation on the other. The article, "Esoteric Buddhism," offers several instances in which Blavatsky's writings failed to meet the standards of academic analysis – for example, in her vast and indiscriminate citations in *Isis Unveiled*, which attest to both "drudgery and misdirected ingenuity"; or in some of the rookie errors of etymology or translation that Müller cites.[117] Beyond critiquing her writings, he also focuses on Blavatsky as a figurehead, speculating that she seemed to have originally been moved by "some strong craving for a spiritual union with the Divine"[118] and was similar to "many people in our time" in being "in search of a religion" beyond conventional faith or religious dogma.[119] We see, here, a tacit acceptance that the spirit of the age included a quest for the truth of religions beyond Christianity – something that Müller himself seems to have identified with, and references graciously as the impetus to Blavatsky's own choices. However, even while allowing for the sincerity of these impulses, Müller suggests that Blavatsky was ultimately forced to rely on trickery and false miracles in order to draw followers: "Madame Blavatsky might have achieved some success if she had been satisfied to follow in the footsteps of Rider Haggard . . . but her ambition was to found a religion, not to make money by writing new *Arabian Nights*."[120] Once more, Müller's *Arabian Nights* analogy stands for the dismissal of a given epistemology as imaginative rubbish. Here, it also equates the work of fiction (à la the imperial potboilers of H. Rider Haggard) with making a quick buck. And yet: What might it mean to take his implication seriously – to place Blavatsky's work in the imaginative space of fiction, despite her encyclopaedic engagement of philological and occultist sources? As we have already discussed, *Isis Unveiled* and *The Secret Doctrine* ultimately block any literal readings by virtue of their methodological excess and arbitrariness. Blavatsky is a writer, after all, who took some of her foundational ideas from *The Coming Race*, which was also a work of genre fiction, if not quite Haggard's *She* or *King Solomon's Mines*. To a more forgiving eye, the implications of Müller's cutting dismissal might include subjecting Blavatsky's writing to a different, less historicist, and more literary standard of reading.

Certainly, he himself is no sympathetic reader of her work or of her personal values. Müller's critique of Theosophical ideas is interwoven throughout with references to Blavatsky's character; he even calls her "a clever, wild, and

---

[117] Müller, "Esoteric Buddhism," p. 771.  [118] Müller, "Esoteric Buddhism," p. 770.
[119] Müller, "Esoteric Buddhism," p. 769.  [120] Müller, "Esoteric Buddhism," p. 775.

excitable girl," who was then misguided into "her later hysterical writings and performances."[121] (In his response, discussed in the next paragraph, A. P. Sinnett remarked with some asperity that "her clever girlhood had ripened till she was close on sixty").[122] Müller goes so far as to attribute Blavatsky's criticisms of his work to pique, writing that "at first she treated me like a Mahatma, but when there was no response I became, like all Sanskrit scholars, a very untrustworthy authority."[123]

Blavatsky, of course, was no longer around to respond to Müller (a thought that perhaps crossed his mind as he wrote his article). Instead, Sinnett put out a rejoinder to Müller in the next issue of *The Nineteenth Century*, which is clearly informed by Theosophical politics. For instance, he seems thoroughly aggrieved by Müller's ascription of "esoteric Buddhism" to Blavatsky rather than to himself. (That choice on Müller's part seems deliberate, considering that Blavatsky mentions Sinnett and his book in the very sections of *The Secret Doctrine* to which Müller is responding.) Sinnett's rejoinder also expresses some of the standard Theosophical challenges to Orientalist authority. He points out that Müller's rejection of "esoteric Buddhism," as an idea completely absent in Buddhist texts, is itself a redundant argument, since "esoteric" is "equivalent to saying there is a view of this subject which is not found in the books."[124] In fact, he entirely dismisses the academic preoccupation with citation and evidence: "[W]hether I obtained the teaching on which *Esoteric Buddhism* rests from a Mahatma on the other side of the Himalayas or evolved them out of my own head need only interest people who begin to be seriously interested in the teaching."[125] (In response, Müller offers sarcastic incredulity: "It is carrying modesty too far," etc.)[126]

The *Nineteenth Century* battle between Theosophy and philology is thus at heart an argument about what counts as authoritative evidence and testimony. Theosophy situates even its most emphatic and absolutist assertions of truth in a larger context of the unknown and the unknowable, referring back to the authority of a mysterious adept or a secret text rather than to verifiable evidence. The further truth claims that Theosophical texts import from Orientalist study or race science find themselves relocated within narratives of the supernatural, which reflect back on the fantasies of kinship and shared beliefs contained within the scholarly or "exoteric" cultural and philosophical analyses. Given these rich fictions, we might see Blavatsky as indeed, at one level, belonging to the order of the *Arabian Nights* – in other words, to the realm of the literary rather than the archival, from within which she is able to insist upon the

---

121 Müller, "Esoteric Buddhism," p. 769.     122 Sinnett, "Reply," p. 1016.
123 Müller, "Esoteric Buddhism," p. 769.     124 Sinnett, "Reply," p. 1015.
125 Sinnett, "Reply," p. 1022.     126 Müller, "Rejoinder," p. 298.

immutable truth value of her texts and theories. The Theosophical approach to the religions of the East may draw from academic Orientalism, may even engage polemically with it and posit itself as an alternative – but it is never interested in settling into a parallel form of study with the same standards of evaluation, one that could be judged according to the conventions and presumptions of philology. It is precisely because they are not parallel, however, that Theosophy and academic Orientalism intersect in such dense, layered, and plural ways.

## 4.2 Echoes and Reflections

The tempestuous codependency of these two cultural formations is thus not simply a matter of Blavatsky's charges, or of Theosophy's debts to Orientalist scholarship and writing; and nor do Max Müller's sarcastic refutations tell the full story of his attitude to theosophical matters. In fact, even though he publicly came out against Blavatsky's conception of esoteric Buddhism, and even as he insisted on the value of verifiable claims, textual expertise, and linguistic training, Müller's pioneering study of comparative religion and comparative philology was motivated by a deep interest in the overlaps in language and religion among cultures, as well as in mystical experiences and syncretic philosophies. In considering the key assumptions and objectives shared by esotericism and philology, then, it is important to look again at Max Müller's scholarship, imbued with its own theosophical spirit.

In an 1882 lecture to candidates for the Indian Civil Services, Müller extolled India as the best place to study comparative philology and comparative religion.[127] As he explained, these particular fields of study equipped their practitioners culturally as well as philosophically.

> All I wish to impress on you by way of introduction is that the results of the Science of language, which, without the aid of Sanskrit, would never have been obtained, form an essential element of . . . an education that will enable a man to do what the French call *s'orienter*, that is, "to find his East," "his true East," and thus to determine his real place in the world.[128]

In offering the idea of "*s'orienter*," Müller reminded his listeners of many things at once: the idea that comparative study and classification offer coordinates through which the student can "determine his real place in the world"; the fact that India was the original locus of this system of study and classification; the fact that there was a career to be made through this study; the idea of "the East" as a fixed relative point in culture, as in nature, that could help "a man" navigate "his" philosophical and worldly education; the idea that, with the study

---

[127] Müller, *India What Can It Teach Us*, pp. 20–21.
[128] Müller, *India What Can It Teach Us*, p. 40.

of such subjects as "the Science of language," each man in the audience could newly discover an East "true" for him; and the fact that India was home to "our nearest intellectual relatives, the Aryans," and so on.[129]

These disparate appeals together form, as if through pointillism, an image of a field and a profession in the process of definition. Along with comparative philology, Müller was one of the founders of the academic discipline he called "the science of religion." The relative newness of the comparative disciplines Müller discusses in his talk explains the contrary pulls and tugs of their multiple aims. Just as Theosophy was still defining itself through manifestos and statements like "The Original Programme," many of Müller's lectures and essays are still negotiating the principle guidelines of these new social sciences. The miscellaneous writings collected in *Chips from a German Workshop* attest to the theosophical motivations of comparative disciplines, often arguing for syncretism as their basis rather than scholarly isolationism and specialization: Orientalism is recognizably a version of what we now call the global humanities. Moreover, Müller's study of comparative religions is transparently motivated by an almost pantheistic desire to locate the perennial, numinous truth shared by all religions. In a lecture on the common source of all religions, for instance, he reflected that "if we will but listen attentively, we can hear in all religions a groaning of the spirit, a struggle to conceive the inconceivable, to utter the unutterable, a longing after the Infinite, a love of God."[130] Theosophical critiques of Müller's work appear to recognize this aspect of his work; on the opposite end of the spectrum, certain linguists even dismissed his theories as "occultist."[131] We see, even as he denounces the Theosophical Society or Blavatsky, that Müller thoroughly endorses other forms of mystical or syncretic religious experience. In a series of lectures in 1892, collected under the name "Theosophy Or Psychological Religion," Müller rejects the sectarian understanding of religion in favor of universal spiritual precepts, and pieces together many principles and approaches shared across religions. He also attempts to reclaim the term made famous (or in his words, "greatly misappropriated") by Blavatsky and Olcott: "one may call oneself a theosophist, without being suspected of believing in spirit-rappings, table-turnings, or any other occult sciences."[132]

---

[129] Müller, *India What Can It Teach Us*, p. 21.     [130] Müller, "First Lecture," p. 12.

[131] Joy Dixon suggests that Müller may even have criticized the Theosophical Society because of the basic shared bond: "Max Müller's own theory of phonetic types had been criticized for relying on 'occult' explanations, and he may have welcomed the opportunity to rehabilitate himself as an academic authority in the wake of Andrew Lang's devastating critique of the mythological, even mystical, elements of his own theories of language" (Dixon, *Divine Feminine*, p. 45).

[132] Müller, *Theosophy*, p. xvi.

Even though Müller rejected the approach of the Theosophical Society, and resented Blavatsky's reach and influence, therefore, he identified himself as a "theosophist." We see this in his ardent interest in personal, heterodox forms of religious experience, as well as in his own belief in a fraternal and syncretic approach to religion that was not ultimately dissimilar to the Theosophical Society's creed of "Universal Brotherhood." In "A Real Mahâtman," an 1896 essay in *The Nineteenth Century* on the Hindu mystic Ramakrishna Paramahansa, Müller praises the truth and wisdom of Ramakrishna's spiritual teachings, the beauty of his "ecstatic utterances,"[133] and what he sees as "most extraordinary," the fact that Ramakrishna went beyond Hindu customs and divinities to love and worship Islam and Christianity, thus demonstrating "how it was possible to unify all the religions of the world."[134] In his excitement over the universality of Ramakrishna's ideas and spiritual experiences (which he presents as emerging, nonetheless, from the very particular style and sublimity of Vedanta), we see the personal passion and search that impelled Müller into his academic work as one of the founding figures of religious studies in the West. Indeed, Ramakrishna's most famous student, Swami Vivekananda – who made his own contributions to the spread of Hindu philosophy in the West at the 1893 World's Parliament of Religions in Chicago and thereafter – described Müller as something of a Mahatma himself, or at least a "silverheaded sage, with a face calm and benign, and … every line in that face speaking of a deep-seated mine of spirituality somewhere behind."[135]

Blavatsky may not have lavished such extravagant praise on Müller, but there were resonances. Esotericist and Orientalist rhetoric seem sometimes to share an uncanny resemblance in this period, when each was codifying the principles of a system of religious study and articulating its motivating ambitions. In a journal article from 1888, Blavatsky clarifies the Society's syncretic attitude toward different religious persuasions quite emphatically: "Theosophy is not a Religion, we say, but RELIGION itself," a statement of essence in line with the claim to represent the perennial wisdom.[136] More surprisingly, a similar impulse may be detected in the discipline of philology; as Max Müller writes, "In the science of language, languages are not treated as a means; language itself becomes the sole object of scientific inquiry …. We do not want to know languages, we want to know language."[137] Here are two comparable comparatisms, motivated by a similar desire to fix the idealized concentrate shared by variable particulars.

---

[133] Müller, "Real Mahâtman," p. 316.    [134] Müller, "Real Mahâtman," pp. 318–319.
[135] Vivekananda, "On Professor Max Müller," p. 280.
[136] Blavatsky, "Is Theosophy a Religion?" p. 14.    [137] Müller, "Science of Language," p. 33.

These grand statements of ambition also explain, indirectly, why Theosophy and philology turned to India as the locus of this essential "religion" or "language." Max Müller writes that the variety of Indian culture allows it to demonstrate, in essential form, "the history of histories, and yet the mystery of all mysteries ... religion."[138] The characteristic rhythm of this formulation, which emphasizes the singular within the plural or the numinous within the particular (a religion/RELIGION, languages/language, histories/history, mysteries/mystery), casts India as the repository of original essences, not only home to Hinduism, Buddhism, and Zoroastrianism but also, ultimately, the very ground of the disciplines of philology and comparative religion.[139] Elsewhere in the talk, Müller returns to the original family of the Aryan hypothesis and the "feeling of closest fraternity which ... changed millions of so-called barbarians into our own kith and kin."[140] Even for the Oxford Orientalist who never set foot on Indian soil, the study of languages and religions is a deeply personal, even familial, exploration, one that crosses past the boundaries of given identity and becomes a means through which to dislodge the assumed categories of the civilized and the barbarian, the self and the other. The Theosophists' interest in the "ancient wisdom" only literalizes these philological truisms, through an alternative history that locates the origin and essence of the Aryans' religion, language, and race in India.

To think of such similarities is not to minimize the significant differences between the content of Max Müller's philology and H. P. Blavatsky's Theosophy: Müller sees the Aryans as originating somewhere in Central Asia, for instance, as opposed to the Theosophists' Aryavarta; as the dispute in *The Nineteenth Century* demonstrated, moreover, Theosophy and philology differed significantly in their readings of various religions, such as the concept of "esoteric Buddhism" that occasioned such a sharp spat in the journal – the fulcrum of which lies in the fact that Buddhism was an anti-caste movement. These specific disagreements stem, as we have seen, from the basic divergence over what might count as authoritative evidence. In his final 1893 rebuttal to Sinnett in *The Nineteenth Century*, Müller objects: "He says that I have no right to speak with authority. I have never claimed to speak with authority . . .. I simply speak

---

[138] Müller, *India What Can It Teach Us*, p. 21.

[139] The full quotation is: "take that which, next to language, has most firmly fixed the specific and permanent barrier between man and beast ... which ... is also the foundation of all national life – the history of all histories, and yet the mystery of all mysteries – take religion, and where can you study its true origin, its natural growth, and its inevitable decay better than in India, the home of Brahmanism, the birthplace of Buddhism, and the refuge of Zoroastrianism ... and why not, in the future, the regenerate child of the purest faith, if only purified from the dust of nineteen centuries?" (Müller, *India What Can It Teach Us,* p. 21). Religion and language thus both affix the identity of "man" as human rather than animal, as well as fixing nationality.

[140] Müller, *India What Can It Teach Us*, pp. 35–36.

with facts and arguments."[141] In reality, both Theosophists and philologists claimed that fact was on their side. Theosophy simply qualified this claim to specify esoteric fact, that which took cognizance of truths and realities beyond the known archives, beyond even the realms of the sensible and the visible.

## 4.3 Theosophical Parables

One compelling test of the interpenetration of these two forms of Orientalism – Theosophy and philology, or the esoteric and the academic – is sadly subjective and unprovable: frequently, sentences from Müller sound as though they may be from texts by Blavatsky, and often, phrases or passages from Blavatsky seem distinctly indebted to Müller. Given these uncanny echoes, however, or even the more general shared framework of comparatism, the most fundamental difference between the texts of Theosophy and of academic Orientalism may ultimately be a matter of style and mode. Despite the ardor and lyricism of Müller's writing at certain moments, or his utopian perception of mutual understanding and cross-pollination among religions, it is possible for the most part to classify him as an academic researcher, analyst, and writer. Despite the absence of such rhapsodic flights, and a determined effort to assert facticity, Blavatsky conversely would appear to a non-Theosophical reader as either an imaginative writer of speculative fiction, or (to a commentator like Müller) a charlatan. The paratextual trappings she borrows from academic method are treated with such scant respect that they begin to seem ornamental, more like motifs within an elaborate fiction than scholarly conventions.

Within Theosophical texts, then, the indisciplines of esotericism remake the disciplines of Orientalism. The patchwork plenitude of Blavatsky's writing juxtaposes her sources in different patterns, alternating in harmonious overlap or discordant clash with one another.[142] A typical deployment of philological sources might look like this: Blavatsky quotes an Orientalist scholar to back a generalization about, say, the mysterious metaphysical essence of esoteric Buddhism; the next paragraph points out, however, that the scholar's conclusions about Buddhism are irrevocably false, since the real explanation of its metaphysics is known only to a few adepts, who have access to esoteric texts that have never been available to Western scholarship; while revealing this esoteric meaning, though, Blavatsky might well return to the philological

---

[141] Müller, "Rejoinder," p. 302.

[142] In editing Blavatsky's writings on Buddhism in *Blavatsky on Buddhism: Interviews, Letters, and Papers,* Urs App puts together a painstaking inventory of the various sources (documented and undocumented) that Blavatsky relied upon in her writings on Buddhism, which he fills out with information about the history of early Theosophy, including the Masters, and a general biographical context.

literature to bolster some specific aspect of the explanation. She occasionally even registers outrage on behalf of the very scholars who she herself attacks at some other point in the text.[143] Nor does the writing represent its contending impulses as the considered exercise of choice: They are usually expressed through an unrelentingly polemical tone that voices either total approbation or total denunciation. A similar contrariness marks Blavatsky's use of other sources, too, such as the spiritualist press that she alternately defends for seeking an alternative to secular materialism, and excoriates for being ignorant of the "actual" workings of the afterlife as explained in the esoteric texts of the Egyptians, Buddhists, and Hindus.

Blavatsky's writings are enlivened by the friction of different forms of authority rubbing up against one another: the textual authority of the scholar or scientist quoted to bolster the legitimacy of Blavatsky's argument, the authority of an occult Master with access to the real meaning of a scriptural extract or religious precept, the authority of actual practitioners of the exoteric faith under discussion, the authority of the mysterious texts that Blavatsky has been fortunate enough to encounter; and so on. Such appeals to authority insist upon a knowledge that is available only to the elect, continuously reasserting its esotericism. At the same time, they combine to back up the argumentative, grandiloquent, boasting voice of the narrator herself, whether in her persona as the compiler of textual wisdom, both scholarly and esoteric, or as the initiate whose testimony is evidence enough for the authoritative narrative assertions. As such, her works model the magpie syncretism that would go on to become a feature of New Age religions in the twentieth century. In many ways, they also anticipate more recent examples of fringe discourse, with their cherry-picked evidence and authoritative testimony, as well as the outright fabrication of texts and sources. But rather than simply rejecting the entirety of Theosophy on account of such concoctions, elisions, and misrepresentations, a more productive approach might be to take cognizance of the ways in which her writing clearly presses the reader in the direction of the unknown, the playful, and the imaginative.

Indeed, the generalized claim to esotericism in Blavatsky's works is always sliding into something more subjective, along with the presence of the unknown; frequently, the question of authority is literally located within the question of authorship. *The Secret Doctrine* is a pseudotranslation that claims to

---

[143] For instance, one of the most frequent targets of her attacks in *Isis Unveiled* is Max Müller, but while discussing earlier Orientalist theories, she writes: "Had Max Müller happened to fall from the sky at that time, among the scholars of the day, and with his present knowledge, we would like to have compiled the epithets which would have been bestowed by the learned academicians upon the daring innovator!" (Blavatsky, *Isis Unveiled Vol. 1*, p. 443).

be glossing an arcane text in the mysterious, occultist script of Senzar; as for *Isis Unveiled*, Theosophists claim that its many quotations were jotted down "astrally," as Blavatsky conjured up virtual scans of the source texts before her mind's eye, and transcribed the relevant sections.[144] This performative, almost deliberately farcical, figuration of the processes of initiation that culminate in Blavatsky's authorship does suggest that Theosophy's most far-fetched moments teeter on the edge of knowing satire. The text's polyphonous assertions of mastery, along with its formal idiosyncrasies and gestures toward all that is as yet unknown, produce a creative discord that unsettles any singular claim to facticity or authority. The effects of this discord do not limit themselves to the narrative voice, but extend to the other sources and authorities named within the text. The exhaustive naming of narrative interlocutors reinforces the sense that Theosophy's encyclopedic vision has compiled its own origins and influences along with those of the entire universe.

Theosophy's stories about its texts – their origins, authorship, and transmission – in fact become figures for the unknowable assumptions and axioms on which all classificatory systems must rest. *The Secret Doctrine*, for instance, refers back to two textual origins: one in the Senzar poem, *The Stanzas of Dzyan*, and the other in a collection of letters from Blavatsky's Masters or Mahatmas to (mainly) Sinnett, in which the Masters M. and K. H. explain Theosophy's evolutionary cosmology.[145] The first few lines of the "Proem" that opens *The Secret Doctrine* describe the manuscript of *The Stanzas of Dzyan* in vivid detail.

> An Archaic Manuscript – a collection of palm leaves made impermeable to water, fire, and air, by some specific unknown process – is before the writer's eye. On the first page is an immaculate white disk within a dull black ground. On the following page, the same disk, but with a central point. The first, the student knows to represent Kosmos in Eternity, before the re-awakening of still slumbering Energy, the emanation of the Word in later systems. The point in the hitherto immaculate Disk, Space and Eternity in Pralaya, denotes the dawn of differentiation.[146]

These direct statements of symbolic meaning are untroubled by further clauses tracing their derivation. Instead, the testimony of the initiate is evidence enough, however stative and opaque ("the student knows to represent") it

---

[144] This is cited in several Theosophical histories and biographies: Olcott has described Blavatsky at work, starting up to read some invisible document and scribble down notes from it (Olcott, *Old Diary Leaves,* pp. 208–209). S. B. Liljegren cites him as saying that when Blavatsky needed specific books, they were brought to her "the astral way," sometimes including destroyed volumes from the Alexandrian library (Liljegren, *Bulwer-Lytton's Novels and Isis Unveiled,* p. 33).

[145] See Godwin, "The Mahatma Letters."     [146] Blavatsky, *Secret Doctrine Vol. 1*, p. 25.

might seem. The opening paragraph's most telling phrase might be "specific unknown process," which could more generally summarize Theosophy's depiction of the esoteric pasts of categories, cosmologies, and theories. Described in the perpetual present tense of a vision, *The Stanzas of Dzyan* comes across as a generic conceit (the theoretical category of "Archaic Manuscript") rather than a particular physical manuscript. The "specific unknown" location and history of the text is diametrically opposed to academic convention: one thinks of Müller's incredulity that Sinnett could offhandedly equate an "esoteric Buddhism" emerging from his head with one originating in the texts of trans-Himalayan Masters. This generic conceit of *The Secret Doctrine* as a quasi-Tibetan, quasi-Hindu epic manuscript, written in an esoteric script and preserved secretly by the Masters in their trans-Himalayan hideaway, clearly attempts to grant Blavatsky's theories a cosmic sanction. And yet, the "specific unknown process" through which the text came into being, or through which it was conjured before the writer's eye, presents the whole business of origins as mythological, a fantastical tale as in the *Arabian Nights*, or a work of speculative fiction like *The Coming Race*.

If we are to take that thought seriously, we must include the work's frame narrative. The Mahatma letters, which were said to be the source of *The Secret Doctrine*'s cosmologies, were said to have reached Sinnett through "precipitation." For most non-Theosophist scholars, the assumption would be that Blavatsky wrote the letters herself, while claiming they came from her Masters. In 1885, representatives from the Society for Psychical Research concluded that Blavatsky was the author, shortly after the "Coulomb affair," in which a disgruntled Theosophical associate revealed that Blavatsky's chambers in Adyar featured concealed doors, allowing for sleights of hand (such as miraculously materializing letters penned by occult Masters in Tibet).[147] These letters can be riveting, not because of the discursive elaborations on various Manvantaras and root races so much as the touch of epistolary fiction included their gossip, anecdotes, and quarrels. For anybody assuming Blavatsky to be their primary author, the letters are self-deprecating and funny: throughout, the shorthand for "Madame Blavatsky" is "Mad. B.," and there are many excessive gestures of exasperation at Mad. B.'s womanly irrationality, willfulness, and immoderate enthusiasms. The humor occasionally extends to the process of "facsimile precipitation" itself, playing with epistolary conventions as if to highlight the bizarre notion of an astral correspondence: "I have your letter of November 19th, abstracted by our special *osmosis* from the envelope at Meerut."[148] There are even instances when the letters quite openly

---

[147] This event is widely described in the literature of Theosophy.

[148] Barker, *Mahatma Letters,* p. 17.

mock the conceit of mail-by-precipitation: one note, for instance, offers a postal address only to add "unless, indeed, you really would prefer corresponding through – pillows."[149] The punctuation wears its comic timing with pride.

Given these elaborate figurations of authorship and transmission, Blavatsky's arguments about Orientalism and race (and the occulted presence of caste) invite a parabolic reading. If we are to try out the notion of Blavatsky as a writer whose works skate off the authorities and texts she cites into the realm of the imaginative and the literary, might one not read *Isis Unveiled* as an allegory of philology's search for its own "Oriental Kabala," the originary protolanguage and protoreligion of the Indo-Europeans? The most noteworthy stylistic innovation wrought through the text is the thickly significant, almost talismanic use of proper nouns that are said to name racial identity: The significance of the noun lies not in its content but in the unknowable histories to which it alludes, or the kinds of mysterious processes through which "Akkadian" proves to mean the same thing as "Brahman."[150] Esoteric history, through the proliferating genealogies that are revealed only to adepts, offers an accounting of the ways in which racial distinctions are not what they seem, and the history of cultural transmission is not what it seems. In Blavatsky's elastic usage, both "esoteric" and "Oriental" become designations for the same thing: the occulted philosophical stock that both runs counter to the established Judeo-Christian traditions, and, at the same time, turns out to be the true root of those traditions. In that sense, "Oriental" is not simply equated with "Indian" or "Chaldean" or "Egyptian" at various points; it can in fact mean a form of "universal" that is anterior to – and within – everything. After describing the paucity of true knowledge about the Jewish and Christian Kabala, Blavatsky writes about the even greater mystery of the Oriental Kabala.

> How much less is definitely known of the Oriental, or the universal Kabala! Its adepts are few, but . . ... Travellers have met these adepts on the shores of the sacred Ganges, brushed against them in the silent ruins of Thebes, and in the mysterious vaulted chambers of Luxor . . .. Historical memoirs have recorded their presence in the brilliantly illuminated *salons* of European aristocracy . . .. They may be found everywhere.[151]

---

[149] Barker, *Mahatma Letters*, p. 11.

[150] In citing Blavatsky's work, it is important to remember that what might be true of one sentence need not hold for another: thus, the fact that she identifies the Akkadians as some form of Brahmin in one place in *Isis Unveiled* by no means suggests that this is a constant throughout her writing. In fact, "Akkadian" is the name given to one of the seven subraces of the Atlantean root race (which immediately preceded the current, Aryan root-race) in *The Secret Doctrine*, and takes on a different significance there.

[151] Blavatsky, *Isis Unveiled Vol. 1*, p. 17.

Here, if "Oriental" means anything, it means the same thing as "esoteric": the name makes reference to a geographic location (the mysterious place where adepts have maintained the oldest of all Kabalas), and yet, that geographical location turns out to be "found everywhere." What we notice alongside these imaginative homologies is the evocation of atmosphere and sensation: The adepts become like members of a secretive fraternity of superheroes, narrative nodes that hold together diverse histories and an infinitely expansive, changeful geography.

## 5 Conclusion

Theosophy's relationship to Orientalist scholarship by no means fractured the master narratives of race and civilization in Victorian culture: In fact, its esotericist reinventions of the Aryan hypothesis imparted an ethnological vocabulary to future occultist formations, with devastating ideological consequences. Whether we turn to Nazi Aryanism or to the development of Hindu supremacist ideologies, it is possible to see the additional, visionary element that came to this discourse through the intervention of Theosophy. The phantasmatic accounts of religious difference and racial evolution in Theosophical writings are more often than not arranged according to rigid, even eugenic, principles of classification. And yet, the extravagant scale of Theosophical ideas magnifies the schisms and illogic of nineteenth-century racial and civilizational taxonomies. The example of Blavatsky's texts confirms that Victorian Orientalism, understood broadly as all Western discourse about India and other parts of the East, by no means spoke in one voice: Instead, its narratives are as disordered, multiplicitous, contradictory, and therefore, as revealing of their originary assumptions as Blavatsky's own highly structured but fissive systems, or her run-ins with academic Orientalism.

The Theosophical approach to method and authorship dislocates the contemporary discourse of religion, race, and caste from the givenness of Orientalism's epistemological framework, and gives voice to doubts about the infallibility of its expertise. It is clear why scholars like Müller would have been so frustrated by the growing reach and influence of Theosophy, given both Blavatsky's gibes against academic Orientalists, and her selective and often seemingly arbitrary use of their work in her writing. Theosophists consistently criticized the posture of authority adopted by philologists and scholars of comparative religion. This comes through not only in Blavatsky's writings, or Sinnett's ripostes to Müller, but even in Henry Steele Olcott's recollections of his Oxford meeting with Müller, where he bristled at Müller's cultural insensitivity in placing a statue of the Buddha on the ground (rather than on an elevation) by his fireplace.[152] Theosophy's objections formulate a prescient critique of the scholarly attitude that Said described almost a century later as "the picture of a learned Westerner surveying ... the passive ... even silent and supine East, then going on to articulate the East, making the Orient deliver up its secrets under the learned authority of a philologist whose power derives from the ability to unlock secret, esoteric languages."[153] Theosophy also seeks to "mak[e] the Orient deliver up its secrets," but it does so while insisting that the East has much to say. Ultimately, the dream of a shared and long-gone past, understood in terms of common languages, races, and beliefs, opens up the dream of a future reunification across differences.

As Said's description of the Orientalist scholar's "ability to unlock secret, esoteric languages" suggests, moreover, esotericism is a part of philology, rather than a rival or anathema approach. It is perhaps this impetus that makes both Orientalism and Theosophy two prototypical and related versions of the global humanities in the nineteenth century. Their vision is syncretic, interdisciplinary, and ultimately interested in tracing the progression of what is shared as well as what diverges across historical, cultural divides. As this Element has attempted to demonstrate, a fuller sense of these vast and significant cultural formations comes not only from piecing together the grand narrative of Western representations of Eastern religions but also from attending closely to the figures and forms through which that narrative is conveyed. What we find is ambiguity and ambivalence, fantasy mixed in with facticity, and an encounter that refuses to settle into singular definitions or identities.

---

[152] Donald S. Lopez, Jr. discusses the encounter in "Orientalist vs. Theosophist," returning to the disagreement around the esotericism (or lack thereof) of Buddhism. As Lopez analyzes it, Müller's response to Olcott's objections – that the placement of the statue at the fireplace was respectful, since the hearth is sacred to Greeks – signifies Müller's view "that the Buddha is a figure of European culture, like a Greek god, and as the newest member of this ancient pantheon from which Western civilisation emerged, he should be worshipped accordingly" (Lopez, "Orientalist vs. Theosophist," p. 41).

[153] Said, *Orientalism*, pp. 137–138.

# Bibliography


Alfred Trevor Barker, ed., *The Mahatma Letters to A. P. Sinnett from the Mahatmas M. & K. H.* (London: Rider, 1948).

Alfred Percy Sinnett, "Esoteric Buddhism (A Reply to Professor Max Müller)," *The Nineteenth Century*, 33.196 (June 1893), pp. 1015–1027.

Alfred Percy Sinnett, *Incidents of the Life of Madame Blavatsky: Compiled from Information Supplied by Her Relatives and Friends* (Cambridge: Cambridge Library Collection, Cambridge University Press, 2011).

Antoine Faivre, *Access to Western Esotericism* (New York: State University of New York Press, 1994).

Bruce Campbell, *Ancient Wisdom Revived: A History of the Theosophical Movement* (Berkeley: University of California Press, 1980).

Carla Risseuw, "Thinking Culture through Counter-Culture: The Case of Theosophists in India and Ceylon and Their Ideas on Race and Hierarchy (1875–1947)," in Andrew Copley (ed.), *Gurus and Their Followers: New Religious Reform Movements in Colonial India* (Oxford: Oxford University Press, 2000), pp. 180–205.

Donald S. Lopez Jr., "Orientalist vs. Theosophist," in Tim Rudbøg and Erik Sand (eds.), *Imagining the East: The Early Theosophical Society* (New York: Oxford University Press, 2020), pp. 37–58.

Edward Bulwer-Lytton, *The Coming Race*, ed. Peter W. Sinnema (Peterborough: Broadview Press, 2018).

Edward W. Said, *Orientalism* (New York: Pantheon Books, 1978).

Edwin Bryant, *The Quest for the Origins of Vedic Culture: The Indo-Aryan Migration Debate* (Oxford: Oxford University Press, 2001).

Erik Reenberg Sand, "The Marriage between the Theosophical Society and the Arya Samaj," in Tim Rudbøg and Erik Sand (eds.), *Imagining the East: The Early Theosophical Society* (New York: Oxford University Press, 2020), pp. 253–272.

Eve Kosofsky Sedgwick, "Paranoid Reading and Reparative Reading, or, You're So Paranoid, You Probably Think This Essay Is about You," in *Touching Feeling: Affect, Pedagogy, Performativity* (Durham: Duke University Press, 2003), pp. 123–152.

Felix Wiedemann, "The Aryans: Ideology and Historiographical Narrative Types in the Nineteenth and Early Twentieth Centuries," in Helen Roche and Kyriakos N. Demetriou (eds.), *Brill's Companion to the Classics, Fascist Italy and Nazi Germany* (Leiden: Brill, 2017), pp. 31–59.

Frederick C. Crews, "The Consolation of Theosophy," *New York Review of Books*, 43.14 (September 19, 1996), pp. 26–30.

Friedrich Max Müller, "A Real Mahâtman," *The Nineteenth Century*, 40 (1896), pp. 306–319.

Friedrich Max Müller, "Esoteric Buddhism," *The Nineteenth Century*, 33.195 (May 1893), pp. 767–788.

Friedrich Max Müller, "Esoteric Buddhism: A Rejoinder," *The Nineteenth Century*, 34.197 (July 1893), pp. 296–303.

Friedrich Max Müller, "First Lecture: Delivered at the Royal Institution, Feb. 19, 1870," in *Lectures on the Science of Religion: With a Paper on Buddhist Nihilism, and a Translation of the Dhammapada or "Path of Virtue"* (New York: Charles Scribner, 1872), pp. 3–28.

Friedrich Max Müller, "Rede Lecture Delivered in the Senate House before the University of Cambridge, on Friday, May 29, 1868; Part I: On the Stratification of Language," in *Chips from a German Workshop Vol. 4* (New York: Charles Scribner's Sons, 1881), pp. 63–110.

Friedrich Max Müller, "Semitic Monotheism," in *Chips from a German Workshop Vol. 1* (New York: Charles Scribner, 1872), pp. 337–374.

Friedrich Max Müller, "The Home of the Aryas," in *Biographies of Words and the Home of the Aryas* (London: Longmans, Green, 1888), pp. 80–127.

Friedrich Max Müller, "The Science of Language One of the Physical Sciences," in *Lectures on the Science of Language: Delivered at the Royal Institution of Great Britain in April, May, and June, 1861* (New York: Charles Scribner, 1862), pp. 11–37.

Friedrich Max Müller, *Chips from a German Workshop Vol. 2* (New York: Charles Scribner, 1872).

Friedrich Max Müller, *Chips from a German Workshop Vol. 4* (New York: Charles Scribner's Sons, 1881).

Friedrich Max Müller, *India What Can It Teach Us* (New York: John W. Lovell, 1883).

Friedrich Max Müller, *Theosophy or Psychological Religion: The Gifford Lectures Delivered before the University of Glasgow in 1892* (London: Longmans, Green, 1893).

Gail Omvedt, *Dalits and the Democratic Revolution: Dr Ambedkar and the Dalit Movement in Colonial India* (New Delhi: Sage Publications, 1994).

Garry W. Trompf, "Theosophical Macrohistory," in Olav Hammer and Mikael Rothstein (eds.), *Handbook of the Theosophical Current* (Leiden: Brill, 2013), pp. 375–403.

Gauri Viswanathan, "In Search of Madame Blavatsky: Reading the Exoteric, Retrieving the Esoteric," *Representations*, 141.1 (2018), pp. 67–94.

Gauri Viswanathan, "The Ordinary Business of Occultism," *Critical Inquiry*, 27.1 (2000), pp. 1–20.

Gauri Viswanathan, *Outside the Fold: Conversion, Modernity, and Belief* (Princeton: Princeton University Press, 1998).

Gopal Guru, "The Politics of Naming," *Seminar*, 471 (1998), pp. 14–18.

Harry Oldmeadow, *Journeys East: 20th Century Western Encounters with Eastern Religious Traditions* (New Delhi: Third Eye, 2005).

Helena Petrovna Blavatsky, "A Few Questions to Hiraf," *Spiritual Scientist*, 2.19 (July 15, 1875), pp. 218–219, 224.

Helena Petrovna Blavatsky, "From Madame Blavatsky to Her Correspondents: An Open Letter Such as Few Can Write," in *Collected Writings of H.P. Blavatsky, Vol. 1* (Adyar: Theosophical Publishing House, 1999), pp. 126–133.

Helena Petrovna Blavatsky, *An Abridgment of the Secret Doctrine*, ed. Elizabeth Preston and Christmas Humphreys (London: Theosophical Publishing House, 1966).

Helena Petrovna Blavatsky, *Blavatsky on Buddhism: Interviews, Letters, and Papers*, ed. Urs App (Wil: UniversityMedia, 2023).

Helena Petrovna Blavatsky, *Isis Unveiled: A Master-Key to the Mysteries of Ancient and Modern Science and Theology*, 2 vols. (Pasadena: Theosophical University Press, 1988).

Helena Petrovna Blavatsky, "Misconceptions," in *Theosophy: Some Rare Perspectives, a Series of Articles by H. P. Blavatsky* (Los Angeles: Theosophy Company, 2004), pp. 1–25.

Helena Petrovna Blavatsky, *The Esoteric Writings of Helena Petrovna Blavatsky: A Synthesis of Science, Philosophy, and Religion* (Adyar: Theosophical Publishing House, 1980).

Helena Petrovna Blavatsky, *The Original Programme of the Theosophical Society and Preliminary Memorandum of the Esoteric Section* (Adyar: Theosophical Publishing House, 1931).

Helena Petrovna Blavatsky, *The Secret Doctrine: The Synthesis of Science, Religion, and Philosophy*, 2 vols. (London: Theosophical Publishing House, 1888).

Helena Petrovna Blavatsky, "Is Theosophy a Religion?" in Editorial Board of Theosophy Trust (ed.), *Theosophy: The Wisdom Religion* (Norfolk: Theosophy Trust Books, 2015), pp. 11–24.

Henry Steel Olcott, *Old Diary Leaves 1875–78: The True Story of the Theosophical Society* (Cambridge: Cambridge University Press, 2011).

Henry Steel Olcott, *Old Diary Leaves 1878–83: The Only Authentic History of the Theosophical Society* (Cambridge: Cambridge University Press, 2011).

Hugh B. Urban, *Secrecy: Silence, Power, and Religion* (Chicago: University of Chicago Press, 2021).

Isabel Wilkerson, *Caste: The Origins of Our Discontents* (New York: Random House, 2020).

Joscelyn Godwin, "The Mahatma Letters," in Tim Rudbog and Erik Sand (eds.), *Imagining the East: The Early Theosophical Society* (New York: Oxford University Press, 2020), pp. 133–156.

Joscelyn Godwin, *The Theosophical Enlightenment* (New York: State University of New York Press, 1994).

Josephine Ransom, *A Short History of the Theosophical Society* (Adyar: Theosophical Publishing House, 1938).

Joy Dixon, *Divine Feminine: Theosophy and Feminism in England* (Baltimore: Johns Hopkins University Press, 2003).

Julie Chajes, *Recycled Lives: A History of Reincarnation in Blavatsky's Theosophy* (New York: Oxford University Press, 2019).

Leela Gandhi, *Affective Communities: Anticolonial Thought, Fin-de-Siècle Radicalism, and the Politics of Friendship* (Durham: Duke University Press, 2006).

Léon Poliakov, *The Aryan Myth: A History of Racist and Nationalist Ideas in Europe* (Kiribati: Basic Books, 1974).

Lynn Hunt, Margaret C. Jacob, and Wijnand Mijnhardt, *The Book that Changed Europe: Picart and Bernard's Religious Ceremonies of the World* (Cambridge, MA: Harvard University Press, 2010).

Martin Mulsow, "Antiquarianism and Idolatry: The Historia of Religions in the Seventeenth Century," in Gianna Pomata and Nancy G. Siraisi (eds.), *Historia: Empiricism and Erudition in Early Modern Europe* (Cambridge, MA: Harvard University Press, 2005), pp. 181–210.

Maurice Olender, *The Languages of Paradise: Aryans and Semites, a Match Made in Heaven* (New York: Other Press, 1992).

Nicholas A. Germana, "Self-Othering in German Orientalism: The Case of Friedrich Schlegel," *The Comparatist*, 34 (2010), pp. 80–94.

Nicholas Goodrick-Clarke, *The Occult Roots of Nazism: Secret Aryan Cults and Their Influence on Nazi Ideology* (New York: Tauris Parke, 2004).

Peter Pels, "Occult Truths: Race, Conjecture and Theosophy in Victorian Anthropology," in Richard Handler (ed.), *Excluded Ancestors, Inventible Traditions: Essays towards a More Inclusive History of Anthropology* (Madison: University of Wisconsin Press, 2000), pp. 11–41.

Peter van der Veer, *Imperial Encounters: Religion and Modernity in India and Britain* (Princeton: Princeton University Press, 2001).

Raymond Schwab, *Oriental Renaissance: Europe's Rediscovery of India and the East, 1680–1880* (New York: Columbia University Press, 1984).

Rita Kothari and Krupa Shah, "More or Less 'Translation': Landscapes of Language and Communication in India," in Yves Gambier and Ubaldo Stecconi (eds.), *A World Atlas of Translation* (Amsterdam: John Benjamins, 2019), pp. 125–148.

Roland Lardinois, "The Idea of Caste through the Ages: Concepts, Words, and Things," in Surinder S. Jodhka and Jules Naudet (eds.), *The Oxford Handbook of Caste* (Oxford: Oxford University Press, 2023), pp. 31–47.

Romila Thapar, "Foreword," in Thomas R. Trautmann, *Aryans and British India* (New Delhi: Vistaar, 1997), pp. xi–xvi.

Romila Thapar, "Multiple Theories about the Aryans," in Romila Thapar, Michael Witzel, Jaya Menon, Kai Friese, and Razib Khan (eds.), *Which of Us Are Aryans?: Rethinking the Concept of Our Origins* (New Delhi: Aleph Book, 2019), pp. 30–93.

Romila Thapar, "Reflections on Looking Again at the Aryan Question," *Social Scientist*, 49.9/10 (2021), pp. 7–18.

Romila Thapar, "The Theory of Aryan Race and India: History and Politics," in *Cultural Pasts: Essays in Early Indian History* (New Delhi: Oxford University Press, 2000), pp. 1108–1140.

Ronald Inden, *Imagining India* (London: Hurst, 2000).

Sten Bodvar Liljegren, *Bulwer-Lytton's Novels and Isis Unveiled* (Uppsala: A.B. Lundequist, 1957).

Stefan Arvidsson, *Aryan Idols: Indo-European Mythology as Ideology and Science* (Chicago: University of Chicago Press, 2006).

Sumathi Ramaswamy, "Occult Losses," in *The Lost Land of Lemuria: Fabulous Geographies, Catastrophic Histories* (Berkeley: University of California Press, 2004), pp. 53–96.

Susan Bayly, "Caste and 'Race' in the Colonial Ethnography of India," in Peter Robb (ed.), *The Concept of Race in South Asia* (Delhi: Oxford University Press, 1995). pp. 165–218.

Susan Bayly, "Hindu Modernisers and the 'Public' Arena: Indigenous Critiques of Caste in Colonial India," in William Radice (ed.), *Swami Vivekananda and the Modernization of Hinduism* (Delhi: Oxford University Press, 1998), pp. 93–137.

Susan Bayly, *Caste, Society and Politics in India of the New Cambridge History of India* (Cambridge: Cambridge University Press, 1999).

Swami Vivekananda, "On Professor Max Müller," in *The Complete Works of Vivekananda, Vol. 4. Ed. 12* (Calcutta: Advaita Ashrama, 1958), pp. 278–283.

Thomas Green, "'The Spirit of the Vedānta': Occultism and Piety in Max Müller and Swami Vivekananda's Interpretation of Ramakrishna," *Numen*, 64.2–3 (2017), pp. 229–257.

Thomas R. Trautmann, *Aryans and British India* (New Delhi: Vistaar, 1997).

Urs App, *The Birth of Orientalism* (Philadelphia: University of Pennsylvania Press, 2010).

Wendy Doniger, "Introduction: Working with Available Light," in *The Hindus: An Alternative History* (New Delhi: Penguin Books, 2011), pp. 17–49.

William Jones, "Third Anniversary Discourse, on the Hindus, Delivered 2d of February, 1786," in John Shore Baron Tieignmouth (ed.), *The Works of Sir William Jones Vol. III* (London: John Stockdale and John Walker, 1807), pp. 24–46.

Wouter J. Hanegraaff, "The Theosophical Imagination," *Correspondences: Journal for the Study of Esotericism*, 5 (2017), pp. 3–39.

# Acknowledgments

I would like to thank the editors of the Elements in the Global Humanities series, everyone at Cambridge University Press who has overseen this project, and its two anonymous reviewers. In particular, this Element would not exist without Malvika Maheshwari, who has been a wonderfully enabling and clear-sighted editor. I am thankful to Harish Sai and Sayali Palekar for their research assistance early in the project, and most grateful to Pourvaja Ganesh for her crucial help at a key stage. Shree Thaarshini Sriraman and Vighnesh Hampapura were invaluable in their insightful feedback and help closer to the finishing line, for which I thank them.

This Element actually began life many years ago at Duke University. In writing it, I have been frequently reminded of the close friendships that sustained me as a graduate student. Most of all, I treasure the memory of working with two extraordinary mentors and teachers whom I can no longer thank in person: to Eve Kosofsky Sedgwick and Srinivas Aravamudan, my deep gratitude.

It has been my good fortune to be at Ashoka University for the last ten years, and I am grateful for its research support. I owe huge thanks to my many comrades and friends (floundering and otherwise) at the university, and to my superlative students at Ashoka over the years. The department of English is a dream home, for which I thank each of my colleagues. Madhavi Menon and Jonathan Gil Harris, in particular, have been an unstinting source of friendship, encouragement, and zing since we started out together. I've enjoyed traveling this road (literally and metaphorically) with Aparna Chaudhuri, and drawn great support from our chats about work and writing. I would also like to thank Rita Kothari, Alexandra Verini, Abir Bazaz, and Saikat Majumdar for their helpful advice at different points along the way.

If I were to name the cherished friends, cousins, aunts and uncles, outlaws, family friends, and other loved ones who have made it possible to thrive and be happy, I would be here from dawn to dusk, miss my deadline, and overshoot the word limit. I will deliver those acknowledgments in person. For now, big and loving thanks to Amitabh Dubey and Amulya Gopalakrishnan. Gratitude and adoration for Noor Dubey Nundy and Nishq Dubey Nundy, who make life joyful and worth living. Everything is, of course, all thanks to my beloved parents, Manjulika and Suman Dubey, including this work, which I dedicate to them.

# About the Author

**Mandakini Dubey** is Assistant Professor of English at Ashoka University, in Sonipat, India. She received her PhD at Duke University in 2003 and has taught since then in the United States and in India. She is currently at work on a book about Orientalist pseudotranslations in the nineteenth century.

Cambridge Elements ≡

# Global Humanities

## Saul Dubow

*University of Cambridge*

Saul Dubow is Smuts Professor of Commonwealth History in the University of Cambridge and a Fellow of Magdalene College, Cambridge.

## Malvika Maheshwari

*Ashoka University*

Malvika Maheshwari is Associate Professor of Political Science at Ashoka University.

## Frisbee C. C. Sheffield

*University of Cambridge*

Frisbee C. C. Sheffield is Associate Professor of Classics in the University of Cambridge and a Fellow of Downing College, Cambridge.

## About the Series

How do we express our common humanity in ways that articulate the things that connect us while also giving due credence to cultural, geographical, social, political, religious and economic differences? What does it mean to be a human being in our increasingly intricate, varied and challenging global contexts? And how might we address the matter of being human, and what that entails, in these same contexts, via the humanities disciplines? It is those key questions that this new series will attempt, however tentatively and exploratively, to answer. The Elements will bring fresh insights to a range of topics which – though worldwide in scope – will also have the solidity of rootedness in the local and the particular. Commonality will be meshed with singularity and distinctiveness. In moving towards fresh understandings of the 'global humanities', the series will try to construct a vision for the humanities that breaks down barriers, rethinks the past, and reimagines the future.

**Published in conjunction with the Global Humanities Initiative of the School of Arts and Humanities in the University of Cambridge.**

For EU product safety concerns, contact us at Calle de José Abascal, 56–1°,
28003 Madrid, Spain or eugpsr@cambridge.org.

www.ingramcontent.com/pod-product-compliance
Ingram Content Group UK Ltd.
Pitfield, Milton Keynes, MK11 3LW, UK
UKHW020327100725
460335UK00029B/171